Life is Like a Horse Race

To Janny

Don Edwards

11/18/2000

Published by The Lexington Herald-Leader Company
Lexington, Kentucky USA

ISBN 0-9624001-8-1

This book is dedicated to
Elaine Edwards

Contents

Big Blue

Buffy Bleugrazz

Celebs

Famous Kentuckians

Horse Biz

Days Gone By

Just Some Thoughts

Kentucky Politics

Old Lexington

Lexington Characters

Send-Offs

Foreword

Every place that we love and call home deserves to have someone with a special talent for describing the way we live. Sometimes it is a poet, a novelist or a historian, and sometimes it is a gifted newspaper columnist. I think of Mike Royko for Chicago (a favorite of mine), Jimmy Breslin for New York, Molly Ivins for Texas, and of course, Lexington's own Don Edwards.

In each case, these writers act as chroniclers for their communities while also offering an original perspective on the wider world. Each one has a distinctive style and tone, of course, but they are all natural storytellers blessed with unusual intelligence, insight and commitment. Don is not as grumpy as Mike Royko used to be, for example, but he is just as fearless and passionate.

Like everyone who has read and admired Don's columns over the years, I am grateful for his enormous contributions to Lexington. He has enriched us with his blend of social and political commentary, his moving stories and humorous anecdotes, his personality profiles and character sketches. Don's love for Lexington and Kentucky is evident in every column and in the many other ways he has given of himself to his community, including his support as chairman of the Bluegrass Boys Ranch and as a chess coach for area schools.

Above all, I am grateful for the wonderful friendship that my husband, Preston, and I have enjoyed with Don and his wife, Elaine Edwards.

Preston and I first got to know Don nearly 20 years ago, around the time of a celebrity roast at the Hyatt Regency Hotel when I had the dubious honor of being the target. Don, ever on the lookout for the rare and unusual, decided to interview Preston about the occasion. He had been warned that Preston could be a difficult interview, but Don is, as I have said, absolutely fearless. He asked whether Preston had been pleased with the roast. "Very," Preston said, and walked away.

Not the most promising beginning, but it was a beginning. If the friendship were a horse race, the line in *The Racing Form* might read "stumbled at start, recovered, gained strength through the stretch." A few years later, in fact, Don and Preston did stage a sort of match between themselves, known as the Milward Cup (jokingly named for Lexington's 174-year-old mortuary). Don challenged Preston to a combined running and swimming competition that was, to their mutual regret, captured forever on videotape.

Don ignored the advice of his trainer and continued to drink Bushmills and smoke cigarettes right up to post-time. Preston abstained for

48 hours, to his lasting glory. Encouraged by loud cheers from his backers and inspired by his trainer's pre-race pep talk, Don broke on the lead and drew further ahead in the early going, but faded in midstretch when Preston's superior conditioning — those crucial 48 hours — carried the day. Everybody left feeling a winner, though, because Preston and Don had survived the race.

Thankfully, Don's column has had more staying power. For us, it has been both fun and funny — such as the time Don had a two-day interview with Derby guest Zsa Zsa Gabor. In preparation, Don memorized the names and dates of her seven husbands. That turned out to be a good thing. Zsa Zsa could not remember them in chronological order, and Don had to remind her.

As an admirer of Don's work, and as his friend, I am delighted that the *Herald-Leader* is publishing Life is Like a Horse Race: The Best of Don Edwards. It will evoke lots of happy memories — and lots of laughter.

You are going to enjoy this book.

— Anita Madden

Anita Madden and her husband, Preston Madden, are co-owners of Hamburg Place, one of Lexington's most famous thoroughbred horse farms. She is renowned for her Kentucky Derby parties and for her civic and charitable activities.

Introduction

A newspaper column is a little essay in a big hurry. Every one of the columns in this book was written on deadline and none was written with the thought of it being reprinted some day. Like the insect called the mayfly, a column is born, grows up, grows old and dies, all in the space of 24 hours.

Then it's time for the next day's paper, and the next column.

This is a collection of about a hundred of these little journalistic may flies. It is less than 5 percent of the columns I have written, but here's hoping it's a good sample.

Journalism has been good to me. It gave me a front-row seat in life, whether the view was Zsa Zsa Gabor going to the Kentucky Derby or the voodoo mountains of Haiti (Zsa Zsa is in here; Haiti isn't).

Most of all, it enabled me to earn a living by writing — the only thing I ever wanted to do in life.

I came out of the gate at newspapers that were produced with manual typewriters and melted lead.

Thirty-five years later, I'm going down the stretch with papers put together by electronic computers, and with many of my column readers on the Internet.

Lexington has changed, too. It is larger and more anonymous than ever.

Growing up in both Southeastern and Central Kentucky helped me see Lexington in two different ways.

Having Kentucky ancestors dating back to 1780 — a mix of small farmers and a Confederate great-grandfather in Madison County who once owned a thousand acres and a hundred slaves — gave me a sense of history, but not a reverence for it.

This has been a good town to write about. I am fortunate to have seen it through many eyes besides my own.

I saw it through the eyes of the newsroom "old-timers" at the *Herald-Leader* when I was young, and through the eyes of the hundreds and hundreds of people that I interviewed over the years.

I saw it through the eyes of friends such as Preston and Anita Madden, to whom I owe a special measure of appreciation.

I saw it through the eyes of my mother, Anna Lee Edwards, who remembers the excitement of going to the Kentucky Theatre and The Canary Cottage restaurant in the 1920s.

I saw it through the eyes of my sister, Anne E. Hammons, who taught at Cassidy School in the early 1950s. It was visiting her that made me want to write about the town.

I saw it through the young eyes of my two sons, Clay and Gentry Edwards, who grew up in the Lexington of the 1970s and '80s.

And through the eyes of my wife's parents, Reece and Mary Jean Michler Holloway, who knew the Lexington of the 1930s, '40s and '50s.

My father, Emmett C. Edwards, was an L&N railroad engineer. He would take me to work with him when I was a boy and let me blow the locomotive whistle at crossings.

The cars and trucks would stop and everyone would watch and wave. Can you imagine how that felt to a child?

It has taken me a lifetime to understand that what I'm trying to do every time I write a column is to sound that whistle once more.

— Don Edwards
1999

BIG BLUE

Around the commonwealth, nothing stirs up conversation like Big Blue. It's hard to find anyone in Lexington, whether native or transplant, who doesn't get excited before the UK-Tennessee football game or who doesn't spend the month of March glued to the television watching basketball playoffs and hoping for yet another national championship. Times may change, but in the Bluegrass the University of Kentucky Wildcats are eternal. Kentuckians simply don't love anything as much as they love their Cats. Consider, for example, Murray Haydon, the world's third artificial-heart recipient. When he got a basketball signed by the University of Louisville team and coach, Haydon replied: "This is nice, but what I'd really like is to have a Kentucky ball."

Go Big Blue.

Monday, April 27, 1992

Kentucky's Creation: A Basketball-size Bang

When the brilliant scientists announced last week that they had found the origin of the universe, something got overlooked.

Right across the street, the average scientists who used to party a lot and get C's in school also had a press conference.

They announced that they had found the origin of Kentucky.

One of the brilliant scientists said his group's discovery was "like looking at God." One of the average scientists said his group's discovery was "like looking at Bubba."

I don't know much about cosmology, but let me try to explain: The big bang did not create Kentucky. Kentucky was caused by what scientists call the "considerably smaller bang."

Fourteen billion years ago, where Gravel Switch is in Marion County, a piece of unknown matter the size of a basketball exploded and expanded in all directions. Scientists say that's why Gravel Switch is in the center of the state.

As the matter expanded, it formed a huge wisp of gas the size of Frankfort. As this hot air cooled, the earliest forms of Kentucky life developed — neutrons, electrons and $4,000 campaign donations clustered together into organic chemical shapes resembling road contractors, lobbyists, politicians and people who want off-track betting parlors.

Next, a primordial ooze that had bubbled for thousands of years burped and produced the earliest forms of Kentucky life support — catfish, beer cheese and banana peppers.

One of the weirdest things about the origin of Kentucky, scientists say, is that it looks like Kentucky might have copied the origin of the universe.

On the CAT (Cosmos Achievement Test), Kentucky had 211 of 219 answers identical to the universe's answers. The odds of that happening are less than one in 100 trillion.

To explain how much a trillion is, we turn to a letter we just got from Rep. Larry Hopkins, who said of the $4 trillion national debt: "If you had opened a business the day Christ was born, stayed open every single day until now ... and lost $1 million every day, you still have over 700 years to go before you will have lost $1 trillion."

Now Kentucky is doing what universes do when they stop expanding. It is collapsing back onto itself.

That's why Tennessee seems so much closer than it used to.

Wednesday, March 25, 1998

UK'S MEMORIAL COLISEUM WAS A STAR IN ITS DAY

Bob Hope walked to the microphone, looked up to the ceiling far away and then looked out at the audience of 11,000 people.

"My," he said, "this is a big barn."

The crowd roared with laughter.

Hope was talking about Memorial Coliseum, but not the coliseum as we think of it today — an old field house auditorium where the University of Kentucky basketball team practices.

Hope was talking about the coliseum of 40 years ago when he made the "big barn" remark during a performance there.

Of all the changes in scale and proportion in Lexington, perhaps none stirs more memories than the change in how it feels to go to Memorial Coliseum.

Its cornerstone was laid in 1949. When it was built, it was one of the great prides of the city.

In its heyday, just to go there was a big deal that you got dressed up for, whether you went to watch Adolph Rupp coach basketball or to listen to Van Cliburn play the piano.

The history of the happenings at the coliseum is a sort of pop cultural history of Lexington in the last half of the 20th century.

Performers such as James Taylor and Carly Simon sang there (she breast-fed their baby son backstage), and lecturers such as cartoonist Al Capp (creator of "Li'l Abner") spoke there.

In between the Chinese acrobats and the Russian ballerinas, there were poignant Kentucky-type moments, too, and not all of them during basketball games.

I can remember watching a UK commencement and seeing a stork-like figure in cap and gown, a figure that looked a foot taller than everyone else, walk across the stage and get his diploma.

Some members of the audience booed him. They were the same fans who once had cheered him on the basketball court.

It was Bill Spivey, a fallen hero from the point-shaving scandal of 1951, the same year that UK commencements began being held in the coliseum.

Sitting in Memorial Coliseum at a basketball game didn't feel the same as sitting in Rupp Arena.

The crowd was only half as large, and the sense of community was more intense, probably because Lexington was a much smaller town in those days.

And there was a solemn note about the place not to be found in larger and more impersonal venues such as Rupp Arena.

The coliseum was, after all, a memorial.

On the concourse walls, you saw the metal stars honoring the dead of World War II; and the faded photos and old silver trophies of long-ago athletic teams.

When the silver market shot up, burglars got the old trophies, and they were never seen again. They were probably melted down.

It was a shame. Their sentimental value was priceless, and the price of silver went back down anyway.

There are people who can vividly remember the first time they set foot in Memorial Coliseum.

They remember the excitement of the days when it was Lexington's new basketball palace and Rupp was its king.

Just as vividly, there are those who can recall the old concert and lecture days when the men wore suits and ties and the women were in their new spring coats over dresses with linen or lace collars.

No one will ever again remember the coliseum in quite that way.

Like the old trophies, those scenes melted down as different decades and different ideas marched along the Avenue of Champions.

Tuesday, October 15, 1996

DOWNTOWN, B.A. — BEFORE THE ARENA

How did Lexington amuse itself before 20 years of downtown slamma-jamma-bury-the-trey?

That's right. The place got by for 200 years without University of Kentucky basketball at Rupp Arena.

Those people must have been doing something downtown.

But what was it?

OK, here they are, fabulous downtown attractions of yesteryear in the age of BB (before basketball):

You could go bowling upstairs at the Congress Bowling Alley in the 200 block of East Main Street.

The Ben Ali Theatre had scary stage shows with names like Professor Zombie and His Voodoo Revue.

Levas' Restaurant with its famous martinis was a place to see and be seen.

Little Enis with his left-handed, upside-down guitar picking was playing the Zebra Lounge.

Celebrities such as Rosemary Clooney could be seen at the Phoenix Hotel.

Movie star Rock Hudson used to sing around the piano bar at the Gilded Cage on East Main.

Automobile showrooms drew crowds in fall. People went downtown to see the new models.

Bookies were all over downtown — particularly in the Drake Hotel on West Short Street.

When famous Hollywood director John Huston came here to shoot a movie, he ate country ham at the Golden Horseshoe on West Main Street, which had a famous mural on its wall that showed actor Don Ameche buying a horse at Keeneland.

There was also a famous mural of pioneer Lexington on the dining room wall at the Kentuckian Hotel on High Street next to the viaduct.

People actually went shopping downtown at department stores such as Purcell's, Wolf Wile's, Mitchell, Baker, Smith and Stewart's.

No downtown restaurant has been more beloved and talked about since its demise than the Canary Cottage.

There were free, unscheduled concerts on the courthouse yard each Saturday when it didn't rain by such noted street performers as Lost John and his one-man jug band.

Town dog Smiley Pete could be seen grinning at visitors on or around the corner of Main and Limestone streets.

The pool rooms on North Broadway were quite entertaining, particularly when patrons were thrown out the front doors onto the pavement as part of an unofficial downtown sport called "bum tossing."

Main Street was a two-way street. This provided a pastime hazardous to pedestrians called "get the jaywalker."

For some reason, there were two sleazy hotels on North Limestone Street called the Emery and the Savoy that police kept raiding. What could have been going on there?

The UK homecoming parade was a big deal downtown and so was every other parade. But grandest of all was when the place got decorated for Christmas.

Some residents simply enjoyed walking up and down Main Street doing something called "window shopping."

And oh, yes. There was once a miniature golf course on East Short Street. Some Lexingtonians were still talking about it years after it was gone.

It really must have been something. Or maybe it wasn't so much after all. Maybe it just seemed wonderful to people because they were young and having fun.

Come to think of it, what DID everybody do before basketball moved downtown?

Saturday, October 19, 1996

A TICKET TO FAIR SEATS?

You will either love this column or hate it, depending on the color of the cardboard in your purse or wallet.

Yes. Once again, we ask: Who gets the tickets? To whom will the good seats go?

In the volcano of babble that has erupted about a new arena for University of Kentucky basketball, have you noticed the one old subject that keeps being avoided?

It's "Who gets the tickets."

Will they be distributed by the ancient king-nobility-and-peasant system? That's where you "donate" money (pay tribute) to the king (UK) and in return you are knighted (get good seats). Meanwhile, the peasants sit in nosebleed seats or stay home in their thatched huts and watch the game on TV.

Or will the tickets be distributed by lottery (as the student tickets already are) so that all taxpayers have the same chance to watch their state university play basketball?

Nobody wants to talk about this. In Lexington, people would rather disclose the intimate details of their sex lives than talk about how they get their basketball tickets.

It's enough to remind you of that old bumper sticker: Kentucky Pervert — Somebody Who Likes Sex More Than Basketball.

Maybe they don't want to talk about their basketball tickets because they had to commit an unnatural act (buy football tickets) in order to get them.

But seriously, folks, does anyone think the basketball court is going to get any larger because UK has a larger arena?

The court, the ball and the players are going to stay the same size. And the human eye is not going to change its anatomy.

What does it matter if you have 25,000 more seats — and they're high-altitude perches from which the game looks like a bunch of dots moving on a postage stamp?

Don't worry about the people in those proposed corporate sky boxes. ("Pass the Wild Turkey, please.") They can watch the action on their private TV sets and maybe even get to touch the hem of the coach's garment before the night is over.

For the non-wealthy fan, which way is the wind blowing? The basketball coach spoke in glowing terms this week of a new arena being built "without taxing anyone ... "

(As if we all weren't already paying taxes to support UK, making possible the athletic department that hires coaches.)

But doesn't that sound like business as usual? Won't a new arena built with private "donations" be a case of who gives the money gets the tickets?

That's the same private-club system now in effect.

"Amen! Give us a fair chance!" yell the people with no tickets.

"Shut up! Stop making waves!" yell the people with tickets.

So throw the peasants some more tickets to a bigger arena and maybe they'll be quiet.

After all, isn't a bad seat at a UK game better than no seat at all?

Well, it depends on your point of view. If you keep staring at the people in the good seats and find yourself wanting to attack them with a chain saw, maybe more bad seats just aren't good enough.

With apologies to George Orwell for paraphrasing Animal Farm, when you boil it down, it looks like a simple case of:

ALL FANS ARE EQUAL, BUT SOME ARE MORE EQUAL THAN OTHERS.

If you don't like this state of affairs, maybe all you can do is sue.

Try to get a judge who doesn't have tickets.

Thursday, March 2, 1995

OK, UK FANS, IT'S MARCH, SO GET TENSE

There might be some places where March is not really a month, but just a space between two other months.

This isn't one of those places. People here "tense up" in March.

With help from a reader, let us explain what we mean by tensing up.

Melissa Watts of Lexington writes that she and her husband, Jim, went to a UK-LSU basketball game at Rupp Arena a few years back.

"From the opening tip, we could sense it would be a 'war,'" she said. "The crowd was deafening and on its feet."

Melissa stood up and cheered, too. She cheered for as long as she could.

Finally she had to sit down and take a breather. The people behind her kept on screaming.

Suddenly something landed in her lap. Instinctively, she reached down and picked it up.

It was a pair of false teeth.

A man behind her had yelled so hard for the Cats that he'd lost his teeth. They had sailed out of his mouth and onto her lap. He reached down and Melissa gave him back his teeth. The game went on and UK won by five.

That guy had definitely tensed up.

And that is what March means to millions of Kentuckians. It means tensing up over basketball. There might be no other state in the union where as many people are as scared of losing a basketball game.

They tense up terribly. Some of them have strokes and heart attacks. Years ago, during a UK-Tulane game in Memorial Coliseum, a pregnant woman at the coliseum went into labor, but refused to leave for the hospital until the Cats were up by 15. That suited her obstetrician just fine — he was at the game, too.

There is no telling what will cause someone to tense up during a game. Once I wrote a column about a man named Jerry Jones. He had played college basketball and 20 years later, he was a sort of folk hero that a lot of his classmates remembered.

They remembered him because his basketball shorts had fallen right off him during a game. That's right, they just fell off — completely. And there he was, running down the floor in his jockstrap. The crowd went wild. But he tensed up somewhat.

Besides tensing up during college games, there is an incredible amount of tensing up during high school basketball. In some Kentucky towns, so many hot-tempered fans turn out that high school athletics are nicknamed "the Friday night fights."

It is worth noting that many Kentuckians go wacko this time of year because their expectations are so high. If their favorite team doesn't "win it all," they think the team hasn't had much of a season and the whole thing is a disgrace that they want to forget about as soon as possible.

All of this pressure starts building during the winter months, beginning in December, at the same time that people are under pressure from the holiday season.

The pressure continues during January and February when people are depressed about the weather and bills and taxes and a million other things.

By March, the last games of the season and the suspense of tournament time have caused people to tense up so badly that their blood pressure blows out a blood vessel or two when somebody fouls on a three-point shot.

Or else they lose their teeth.

If you are sitting at a basketball game and a glass eye lands in your lap, you'll know it's time to start yelling.

Friday, March 29, 1985

IN KENTUCKY, BASKETBALL CLINGS TO THE CONSCIOUSNESS

"This is nice, but what I'd really like to have is a Kentucky ball."
— Murray Haydon, the world's third artificial heart recipient, upon receiving a basketball autographed by the University of Louisville coach and team.

No problem. Murray Haydon got his basketball autographed by the University of Kentucky Wildcats.

All it took was a telephone call to outgoing UK coach Joe B. Hall's office.

Hall and his team autograph about 4,000 basketballs a year for Kentucky fans, balls that are auctioned at charity events and awarded as prizes in contests.

The supply never meets the demand. But a special exception can always be made for a man whose plastic heart beats in rhythm to a dribble on a hardwood floor.

Because basketball is the dream game in Kentucky, the stuff of legend, the stuff of myth.

And the dream shapes reality. It causes people to do things they ordinarily wouldn't do — such as in Lexington, where developers Don and Dudley Webb built the Radisson Plaza Hotel so that the city could serve as host for the NCAA Final Four this year.

"The NCAA had turned us down before," recalled Dudley Webb,

"because we didn't have enough hotel rooms within walking distance of Rupp Arena. So we played a finesse move when the NCAA search committee came to town. We hired a couple of bulldozers to move earth around and we put up project signs. It showed commitment and it worked.

"Then Don and I looked at each other and we knew: Now we've got to build it.

There's no doubt in my mind that we probably wouldn't have built that hotel if it weren't for basketball."

For the 41-year-old Dudley Webb, it was, in a sense, a decision he and his brother had been heading toward all their lives. Their hometown was Whitesburg in Eastern Kentucky and they have been UK basketball fans "since we were old enough to listen to the radio. We grew up listening to Kentucky basketball, just like most mountain kids."

A few miles away from the hotel the Webbs built is 2,000-acre Hamburg Place horse farm, where five Kentucky Derby winners have been foaled. Here each year, Anita and Preston Madden host the state's most famous Derby Eve party, an internationally known extravaganza where Hollywood movie stars rub elbows with millionaire horse buyers.

For the first time, the huge Madden party tent went up a month early this year. Basketball was the reason. The Maddens are playing host to a media party for about 1,500 people in conjunction with the Final Four.

"I'm sure I wouldn't do this for anyone else," said Mrs. Madden, who played on the girls' basketball team and was a cheerleader for the boys' team during her high school days in Ashland. "But the Final Four is so special and so exciting."

Why is basketball so important to Kentuckians? Ask a fan.

On the night of March 16 in Salt Lake City, 71-year-old Steve Rardin watched UK play the University of Nevada-Las Vegas.

It was a personal milestone for Rardin — the 500th consecutive UK basketball game that he had attended. From Alaska to Japan, Rardin, who owns a Lexington magazine-distribution company, has been following the UK Wildcats for 50 years.

Ask him why basketball is important to Kentuckians and his answer is: "It's the tradition. It goes back to the high schools. Even in the hard old days, most any school could find five boys who could play the game."

And that's where the story of Kentucky basketball begins — with bad roads and empty pockets.

When Dr. James Naismith invented the game in 1891, it was made to order for a predominantly rural state like Kentucky. It could be played indoors or outdoors, it was inexpensive and it was fun.

Those were paramount considerations for many Kentucky schools, for the history of the state is the history of bad roads. Citizens had to be within easy traveling distance of a county courthouse to conduct the everyday affairs of life. If a community wasn't, it petitioned the state to subdivide it into a new county so that it could build its own courthouse.

This led to Kentucky having 120 counties. Only two U.S. states — Texas and Georgia — have more. And every Kentucky county had one or more schools. This was the grass-roots foundation for organized competitive athletics.

But many of those tiny rural schools had empty pockets. They couldn't always afford football fields and baseball diamonds, equipment, uniforms and road trips.

Basketball was affordable. It could be played in a YMCA gym, a tobacco warehouse or even under a tree with a hoop nailed to it.

Dr. Naismith's 1891 invention was being played by college students in Kentucky before the turn of the century, but more as an exhibition or amusement than as a major sport.

In the early years of the 20th century, basketball came into its own in Kentucky, gradually sweeping the state over the next three decades. The kids who learned the game in high school — in farm towns, in mining camps, in cities — took their enthusiasm on to college.

The UK program had begun in 1903, with the players chipping in money to buy the ball. It was hardly a dramatic beginning. In UK's first five seasons, the team won only 10 of 35 games. By the 1911-12 season, however, the basketball Wildcats (a nickname first used for the football team in 1909) went 9-0 and were the Southern Champions.

Those were Kentucky high school basketball's important formative years, too.

And by 1918, high school basketball had its own athletic association and an annual tournament in Lexington. Out of this would come a Cinderella story that was a sportswriter's dream — the Carr Creek team of 1928-29.

It was a team that is as legendary in Kentucky high school basketball history as coach Adolph Rupp's 1948 "Fabulous Five" is in Kentucky college basketball history.

The Carr Creek players, wearing mismatched uniforms, came from an isolated mountain village of 140 population, a place so small that it was 20 miles from the nearest railroad — but they went all the way to the national high school tournament in Chicago.

The *Chicago Tribune* wrote that "no town anywhere ever had a team which has captured the imagination and hearts of basketball fans everywhere as have these lithe sharpshooters whose uniforms were overalls and whose school is a barn-like structure with its front porch digging into a mountainside."

Carr Creek didn't win the national tournament, but another Kentucky high school, Ashland, did — 20 years before UK won a national championship. Ashland had beaten Carr Creek in a four-overtime game that year in the state championship.

It fired an enthusiasm for high school basketball that still continues in Kentucky. The annual high school tournament, nicknamed "The Sweet Sixteen," is so strongly supported by fans that Kentucky holds the world's record for the largest crowd (more than 20,000) ever to attend a high school basketball game.

UK, the state's largest university, had built good teams through the 1920s and 1930s, emerging as a major basketball power. And coach Adolph Rupp had gradually gained national recognition that was sealed into immortality after World War II with Rupp's Fabulous Five of 1948, a team that won the first of UK's five national championships and also won the gold medal at the Olympic Games.

Rupp went on to become the winningest college coach in the history of the game. And other state universities eventually built their own dynasties over the years, such as coach Ed Diddle's teams at Western Kentucky University and, more recently, coach Denny Crum's teams at the University of Louisville.

In the early years, radio broadcasts put basketball games within the reach of even the most isolated Kentuckians. Beginning in the 1950s, television did the same.

Even football coach Paul "Bear" Bryant gave up a coaching job at UK in 1954 because his program simply couldn't compete with Rupp's program. The popularity of basketball in Kentucky is more than enormous. It is supreme.

The bad-roads-and-empty-pockets story explains how basketball became so popular in the state, but there is a deeper meaning in why basketball is so important to Kentuckians.

One answer is buried in the history of the state's development. Kentucky has traditionally been an agrarian state. The rapid industrialization of the 19th century scarcely touched it. At a time when Chicago, St. Louis and other cities were raising skyscrapers, Kentucky was still raising horses and tobacco.

Had Kentucky developed an industrial metropolis of its own, there would have been major professional athletic teams to go along with it. But it didn't.

Thus, basketball became, in a sense, the only game in town, a game of undivided loyalty.

Another answer lies in geography. Kentucky is a fragmented state. Regions are sharply divided, such as the lush Central Bluegrass portion of aristocratic horse breeders and the mountainous Eastern portion of Appalachia. Or the spreading farmland of Western Kentucky and the border urban areas of Louisville and Northern Kentucky, which grew up around Cincinnati.

Basketball — particularly UK basketball — is the only sport that has unified the state.

Horse racing, despite its glamour and glitz, despite its world-famous Kentucky Derby, could never do that. It was the "sport of kings," the game of the affluent. It had its own tradition that the average Kentuckian could share in, but never be at the center of — only the wealthy could afford a horse farm or a racing stable. But basketball was the people's game — blue collar, white collar or no collar. It belonged to everybody.

And then there were the questions of pride and shame.

At the time that basketball began capturing hearts and minds in Kentucky, the state's national image was a holdover from the Civil War. It was a confusing image, a mishmash of mint-julep-sipping Kentucky Colonels raising Derby winners on the old plantation and Hatfield-and-McCoy-type feuding mountaineers raising hell by guzzling moonshine and murdering one another.

This was, after all, the state that had begun the 20th century by assassinating a governor, a shameful mark that made it unique among the other states.

Basketball gave Kentucky favorable national recognition. It gave Kentuckians something to be proud of at a time when they needed it.

When the Ashland and Carr Creek kids went to Chicago in 1928, it proved to Kentuckians that their kids could be the best in the country. When Rupp's Fabulous Five won the Olympics in 1948, it proved that Kentucky could be the best in the world.

Big-time athletics is a heady drug. In Kentucky, basketball developed into monomania — with powerful, unrelenting pressure on coaches and players to continually repeat the triumphs of the past.

State historians have warned of the dangers of the monomania. They have pointed out that having a winning basketball team cannot compensate for Kentucky's low national ranking in education. Their voices are consistently drowned out by the roar of the crowd as the latest season's All-America hero slam-dunks the ball.

Basketball is so deeply rooted in the Kentucky consciousness that it is a torch passed without question from one generation to the next. Or, as NBC commentator Al McGuire once put it: ". . . the kids in Kentucky start listening to the games on the radio when they are still being burped on their fathers' shoulders."

Small wonder, then, that to Kentuckians, the Final Four finally coming to Lexington — smack in the center of a state that has loved the game, fought for its place in it, cherished its honors and yearned for more — is an event of once-in-a-century magnitude.

They will be talking about it for as long as they talk about basketball.

And in Kentucky, that's forever.

Friday, December 8, 1989

■ When Rick Pitino became the University of Kentucky's basketball coach in 1989, some Kentuckians had trouble understanding his accent, and this, of course, became the topic of much conversation.

COACH, CAN YOU SAY THAT AGAIN . . . IN ENGLISH?

"But what if I meet him sometime and have to talk to him?" asked Bobby Gene. He sounded as nervous as a coup leader in Manila.

"You're going to have to face this sooner or later," I said. "He's the most popular Yankee in Kentucky since before the Civil War."

"I know all that," Bobby Gene said. "And I love to go down to Rupp and see them run 100 miles and shoot 300 times a game. But what if I have to talk to him?"

"Well, what if you do?"

"Well, that's the point. What if I can't understand what he says and he can't understand what I say? I'll look like a fool."

"OK, let's go over it again. What are sinna, ford and god?"

"I got that part. Those are the team positions. Center, forward and guard."

"See? It's easy. He's a regular person like you and me. He just has a different accent."

"Listen," said Bobby Gene, "I've tried to talk to some of them before and they aren't exactly like you and me. They think corn is only a vegetable and not also a bread."

"OK, what else are you having trouble understanding?"

"That 'hots' stuff."

"What do you mean?"

"Like on those TV commercials he does. There he is, saying, 'Kentucky basketball has always had a special place in the hots of Kentuckians . . .' "

"He means 'hearts' — that's all."

"And even the TV commentators are starting to talk that way. What's all this 'duh-dee duh-dee' they keep saying?"

"They mean 'the D' — you know, defense."

"Then why don't they say, 'the D' like they used to?"

"I guess the way any new coach talks is bound to have some effect on the people around him."

"I'll say it does," said Bobby Gene. "Remember those post-game coaches' interviews when 'athlete' used to be a three-syllable word? Now they've taken the 'uh' out of the middle. "

"It never really had three syllables, Bobby Gene."

"Well, maybe not. But at least you could understand what they were saying."

"You're just going to have to make this adjustment."

"I think the university ought to help out people like me," said Bobby Gene.

"What could the university do?"

"It could offer a course called Noo Yawk 101 or something so we could learn to talk that way."

"Look, everything's fine. The Big Blue can't get along without us — you know why?"

"Why?"

"Because we're ordinary fans. And the ordinary fan is the hot and soul of college basketball."

"Will you quit that?" said Bobby Gene.

Friday, May 9, 1997

■ Rick Pitino left the University of Kentucky in 1997 to become head coach of the NBA's Boston Celtics. That his successor, Tubby Smith, was UK's first black head basketball coach was just one sign of the many changes Pitino wrought on the basketball program — and on the Bluegrass.

PITINO BROKE INTO BUBBAVILLE

University of Kentucky basketball coach Tubby Smith.
Anyone feel culturally threatened by that?

Anyone afraid of a black head basketball coach at Big Blue?

Before Rick Pitino, the very idea would have generated a whispered subtext of private debate ("Are we really ready for THAT?") in a town with two Confederate statues on the courthouse lawn.

After Pitino, it's different.

The whole sense of possibility is different.

Pitino changed Kentucky more than Kentucky changed Pitino.

That's why the level of sensibility has changed, too.

The fact that the Tubby Smiths of the world, skin color included, can be on a UK short list is partly because of Pitino.

Success brings influence. Style changes tone.

Pitino is great at what he does for a living. A lot of people also think he's an egomaniac with a vacuum cleaner for picking up money.

But one thing is certain:

He's the most popular Yankee in Kentucky since the Civil War.

He was the break in the chain of good-ol'-boy-type coaches.

The fans loved him, Noo Yawk Eye-talian ax-cent, Armani suits and all.

They loved him for a simple reason. They loved him because he was even a bigger basketball junkie than they were and they could feel it in their hearts.

Forget basketball as a game for a moment. Forget the overworked adjectives and the calculated sentiment and the desperate Oh-please-God-let-us-win-this-one-mindset.

Stop thinking of it as sport, just for a moment.

Think of it as a cultural phenomenon, a metaphor for who we are in Kentucky.

Pitino's most enduring legacy in Kentucky won't be the "Paul Milluh" Ford commercials or the autographed basketballs, books and posters.

It won't be the GQ-magazine-cover-"I'm-even-bigger-than-The-Program" attitude.

It won't be the SEC titles or even the NCAA championship trophy.

Or even the $70 million deal that Dan Rather talked about on the *"CBS Evening News"* on Tuesday.

It will be that sense of possibility he's leaving behind him.

He took an old, worn-out tradition and he left something new in its place.

Oh, yes he did.

Come out of denial, "storied-tradition" die-hards.

Here's your storied tradition — two national championships in 40 years and Pitino won half of them.

He didn't mind playing five black starters or having a black woman assistant coach or putting a little fun in place of a Big Blue neurosis ("no win = no self-esteem.")

Even with all that, Pitino couldn't escape the cultural wars.

If a settlement is reached and open-court testimony is never heard in that gender-discrimination lawsuit filed by a female former trainer, it'll be because UK doesn't WANT it to be heard.

The program still has a shield of secrecy in front of it, an air of "insider trading" hanging around its ticket distribution.

If you want to find out who has the good tickets to the games, you have to take UK to court to get the list. That's too much secrecy for what amounts to a state agency that the rest of us support with our taxes.

Even Rick Pitino hasn't changed that. Maybe nobody is going to completely change Bubbaville.

But good luck to him in Beantown.

Thursday, February 11, 1999

Everybody Wants to Be Tubby

What's it like living in a state with 3.7 million basketball coaches?
Like this:

Everybody knows they can't be Scott Padgett or Wayne Turner. But everybody thinks they can be Tubby Smith.

Before that, they thought they could be Rick Pitino, Eddie Sutton, Joe B. Hall and Adolph Rupp.

It's a Kentucky tradition. And it creates a language that enables Kentuckians who don't know one another from a load of coal to communicate in a special way.

Call it Bluespeak. It can be learned as a second language, but for many of us, it's a first language. Here's how it works:

First you quickly say the official Bluespeak greeting, which sounds like a 15-letter word in the form of a question:

"How'boutthemCats?"

(If the other person doesn't immediately respond, he or she might be from Cincinnati or some other foreign country — or might even be a Louisville fan. Go to the next person.)

When the other person responds, it will be by saying something that sounds like two humongous words:

"TubbyneedstotellTurnertoCREATEtheshot, notalwaystakeit."

Then you slow the cadence down and say something like:

"OK, but it's better they're in a slump now than in March. But if it goes on much longer, they may not get out of it by March."

And the other person says something like:

"Yeah, but if it's over too soon, they may have time to get in a whole new slump by March."

Then you say: "Well, we got spoiled and started thinking we owned the Final Four and now we want our NBA farm team back."

Then the other person says, "Look at who we've lost," and starts naming former players.

Then both of you sort of lean your mental elbows on your thoughts and start to settle in for a substantial Bluespeak conversation.

"How far you think they'll go this time? The Elite Eight?"

"Sweet 16. They've beaten seven in the top 25. They ought to be good for the 16."

Then a third person comes up and says: "I think Tubby has over-achieved with what he's got."

Then the first person says: "Losing to 'Bama is overachieving?"

Then the second person says: "Well, here's what I think ... etc. ..., etc."

Once it hits this vein, the talk can go on for minutes or hours or until somebody finally utters a closing sentence like:

"Well, it'll be interesting to see what happens."

"Yeah, it sure will. Go, Blue."

And it's over.

Nobody has ever done a study to see how time devoted to Bluespeak affects productivity in the Commonwealth.

On the other hand, what a morale builder. If you want to see Kentuckians energized, offer them a chance to win basketball tickets.

It's hard to blame fans for all thinking they're coaches.

The idea of coaching is simply irresistible. Even Adolph Rupp couldn't give it up.

After he was forced to retire at age 70, Rupp continued to have his own TV show competing against the new coach's Joe B. Hall Show.

The new University of Kentucky Basketball Museum in the Civic Center Shops is expected to draw 150,000 visitors the first year.

One thing's for sure. They'll all be coaches.

Saturday, October 26, 1996

■ When it fired head football coach Bill Curry in 1996, the University of Kentucky had to pay Curry $610,000 for the remainder of his contract.

THE MADNESS OF PAYING SOMEONE NOT TO COACH

If the University of Kentucky is going to pay its fired football coach $610,000 for not coaching football for two years, it seems like the least he could do is hang around the stadium after games and help the working custodians pick up paper cups and stuff.

Shouldn't he do SOMETHING for all that cash?

Somebody once said that the precise quality of madness is that it is unaware of being madness.

Perhaps a future historian will look at the 1990s and wonder why there were so many poor Kentucky kids who didn't have money for college — but the state's largest university had $610,000 to pay a man not to coach football.

Is that not madness? If the UK athletic department has that kind of money to throw away, why is UK always asking for more money?

Any other state agency that paid a contractor 610 big ones NOT to provide goods or services would be investigated by a grand jury and ought to be.

Oh, yes, we must be competitive. And football coaches are expensive.

It's a good thing that Kentucky was competitive in the contract field. It wasn't competitive on the playing field.

UK was so charitable toward its gridiron opponents that sometimes it was hard to tell whether it was a football team or the United Way.

We didn't have to pay a coach $305,000 a year to lose games. There are millions of people who would have lost games for, say, $50,000 a year.

The $255,000 saved could have been used to throw a party as compensatory damages for Kentuckians who got ulcers and clinical depression from watching UK football.

Everybody knew that the price of work had been rising. But who would have thought that the price of non-work had gotten so high?

Maybe UK needs to advertise for bids on not coaching football. There are probably people willing not to do the job for a lot less.

This would all be comical if we didn't have a university where coaches are paid 10 times as much as teachers and students go to class in old buildings while the basketball coach beats the drum for a new arena.

Why don't the UK president and the governor stand up on their hind legs and say which is really more important — education or basketball?

Maybe they're afraid of the basketball coach because he's more popular than they are. After all, he won a national championship.

The football coach didn't win enough games to keep his job. There he goes, kicked out of the Big Blue blimp — but with a $610,000 golden parachute so that he will have a soft, fuzzy landing and disappear.

Collegiate sport is not evil, but it has become big-money entertainment in places like Kentucky, and the way it is administered is questionable.

Wouldn't it look a little strange if UK's chemistry department had a For Sale sign hanging on the door?

And yet that's the situation with the athletic department where the best tickets to the games are pandered to the highest bidders as if they were private property instead of public property.

Any other state agency that routinely discriminated against so many taxpayers would find itself in big trouble.

Kentucky hasn't produced a president since Abraham Lincoln or played a pivotal role on the national stage since the Civil War.

Basketball gave us something to be proud of at a time that we desperately needed it. Football tried to do the same, but failed.

How we run both needs a public accounting. Does anyone have the guts to do it?

Thursday, September 25, 1997

LEXINGTON HAS THAT "FOOTBALL TOWN" FEEL AGAIN

Some of us thought we might never see it again in our lifetimes.

Our children's lifetimes.

Our GRANDchildren's lifetimes.

Lifetimes? It took only about three weeks.

Suddenly, like a bolt of cultural lightning from the Big Blue sky, one of the biggest shifts of consciousness in Lexington in nearly half a century has occurred:

The place is starting to feel like a football town again.

It's almost as if the Saturday-morning ticket scalpers were back in the lobby of the Phoenix Hotel.

It's almost as if the shuttle buses were still running from Main Street to McLean Stadium at Stoll Field.

It's almost as if the crayon-colored autumn leaves, the letter sweaters, and — most of all — the folk heroes of 1951 have somehow been morphed into 1997 on the Internet and downloaded onto the whole town.

That's how far back you'd have to go to find the popularity equivalent of Hal Mumme and Tim Couch.

Yes, there were other colorful coaches and players of more recent vintage.

For example, Fran Curci — dubbed "Mr. Sea 'n' Ski" for his cool shades and glossy mane — and running back Sonny Collins, who broke records and tradition with shaved head and huge blue wig.

But when you're talking Mumme and Couch and historical parallel, you have to go back to the "Bear" and the "Babe":

Coach Paul "Bear" Bryant and his All-America quarterback Vito "Babe" Parilli.

They and their teammates upset Oklahoma 13-7 in the Sugar Bowl on Jan. 1, 1951, and became Kentucky legends for all time.

Parilli was every Saturday's hero back then. A former mayor of Lexington, Jim Amato, probably said it best in 1985 during a Parilli visit here. Amato said:

"Sometimes I can't remember what happened last month, but I've got a hundred pictures in my mind of plays the Babe made — pictures as clear as day."

Bryant called Parilli "the greatest fake-and-throw passer I've ever seen."

Thousands of Kentucky kids had the quintessential Parilli picture cut out of the newspaper and pinned to the wall of their room.

It was a UK publicity photo. It showed the Babe airborne, his legs in an upside-down V shape.

He wore no helmet and his wavy hair glinted in the sunshine. One arm was holding the pigskin behind his head, ready to rocket it into the end zone.

"Well, that's the way we did it in those days," he told me in a 1993 interview. "If you do it that way today, they'll kill you.

"I wasn't a real tall guy. I was only about 6-1. If I had to throw over somebody, I had to get up there."

Couch throws over a lot of somebodies and is breaking records. Mumme has been riding a huge wave of popularity since the season began.

Everybody is talking about them, even though nobody really expects them to beat Florida on Saturday.

It's just the way people used to talk about Parilli and Bryant in tones of hope and excitement.

This is such a positive change from previous seasons, when fans were more like lemmings rushing to the edge of a cliff, that it's bound to be good for Lexington.

That's how folk heroes are born in the Commonwealth. If Mumme and Couch keep winning games, they'll be legends, too.

Maybe the only thing missing from the past is former governor and Big Blue booster A.B. "Happy" Chandler singing "On, On, U of K" over a PA system.

Wednesday, September 9, 1998

FOOTBALL'S RETURN BRINGS MEMORIES OF OLD UK HAUNTS

It's another football season in Lexington, a community where 60,000 fans are ready, willing and able to pack a stadium for a 5-6 season.

Sometimes I miss the old University of Kentucky Experimental Farm, part of which was where Commonwealth Stadium stands today.

It was the last big farm left inside Lexington that I can remember. There were some on the edges of town, but the UK farm was smack inside the city.

Completely surrounded by streets and whizzing traffic, it was an agrarian island in a sea of urbanism.

Driving past the farm on South Limestone Street, you could glance over and see long rows of beautiful flowers where seed varieties were being tested.

Commonwealth is a far, far cry from old McLean Stadium and Stoll Field, which were across from the Paddock Restaurant, a popular college hangout that once stood at Euclid and Rose streets.

In the late 1960s, University of Kentucky students had a saying: "The Greeks go to the Two Keys; the freaks go to the Paddock."

It was not an absolute, but there was much truth in it.

You could see a lot of carefully groomed fraternity and sorority members at the Keys, but if you were looking for long-haired hippies (and undercover narcs), the Paddock was the place to go — "hippie headquarters," as some of its regulars called it.

Well, the Greeks outlasted the freaks (symbolically, anyway).

The Keys is still standing at 333 South Limestone, but even the old Paddock building is gone. The site was redeveloped, and a Baskin-Robbins store is there now.

Hippie headquarters moved north to downtown at a restaurant-bar called The Clubhouse at East High and Rose streets.

Later the name of the bar was changed to High on Rose. The business is long gone, but the vacant building is still there.

Today only the ghosts are playing Janis Joplin and Jimi Hendrix on time's imaginary jukebox.

On a football game day back then, so many out-of-town fans were staying downtown that shuttle buses started from the middle and east end of Main Street instead of from the west end, where the hotels are today.

Fans were staying in places such as the Phoenix Hotel and the Downtowner Motel.

If I had a quarter for every football ticket scalped in the lobby of the old Phoenix, I would be enjoying the sunset on Maui right now instead of writing this column.

A lot of people walked to the stadium back then. There was no official tailgating site — no space for one — but there was what might be called "portable tailgating."

Many a half-pint bottle and pocket flask made it past the entry gates and into the stadium.

McLean Stadium bore no resemblance to the pigskin palaces of today.

The stadium was old and kind of dirty looking compared to the bright and clean Commonwealth.

McLean attracted a cross-section of Kentucky humanity. Being alive itself, the stadium added vitality to downtown merely by being a few blocks from Main.

Since the UK farm turned into gridiron and became part of the Big Blue 'burbs, football in Lexington hasn't had the same feeling as it did on Stoll Field.

It's a suburban sport now.

But one thing hasn't changed. The two most-heard words this time of year aren't "love" and "money" or "death" and "taxes."

They are:

"GO BLUE!"

BUFFY BLEUGRAZZ

Every April and October, it's time to go to Keeneland. Time to skip work, bask in the sunshine, place a few bets, lunch on beer and burgoo and watch sleek thoroughbreds speed their way around America's most beautiful racetrack. All this is just a backdrop, though, for Keeneland's really big sport — eyeing other people in the clubhouse and what they wear. Nobody does this better, of course, than Don Edwards' "pseudonymous social arbiter, Buffy Bleugrazz, and her rural cousin, Barbara Jean." Who cares about checking the morning line? Would anyone dare head to Keeneland without adhering to the latest fashion guidelines of Buffy and Barbara Jean? As Buffy would say, "It would be terrible, darling."

Friday, May 4, 1990

DERBY GALAS: SURVIVAL OF THE CHIC-EST

The great weekend was here at last — parties, horses, money, glamour, excitement and a chance of rain.

It was time to seek out our pseudonymous social arbiter, Buffy Bleugrazz.

We found her wrapped like a mummy in one of those Romeo Gigli creations, looking as excited as Rob Lowe with a videocam.

"O chic one," we implored. "Enlighten us about the greatest annual sporting spectacle of the uncommon wealth of the Commonwealth of Kentucky.

"In other words, tell us about the Derby."

She tapped a sculptured nail on her Rolex and considered her answer.

"Well, darling," she began, "if your horse farm made less money than your caterer did last year, you probably can't afford to have a party."

"But won't people have Derby parties anyway?"

"Of course. They have no choice. They have to entertain their bankers with the money they've borrowed."

"What is a good topic of conversation this year?"

"Furs, jewels and face lifts are out, darling. Try something new like: 'Did you hear the Japanese bought the Iwo Jima statue and they have a few changes in mind for it?' If that doesn't work, smile a lot and try to guess who's wearing rented clothing."

"Suppose you have too many juleps and behave outrageously."

"Explain that you went temporarily insane from eating airline food."

Since Buffy has seen more traffic on life's highway than Interstate 75, we asked her for a social guidebook to the Derby.

Naturally, she obliged.

Buffy loves to give advice. It isn't always right, but it's always free.

And so, here they are, darlings — Buffy's top 10 tips on how to survive the big, chic weekend:

10. Never go to any Derby party where the average age is deceased.

9. Don't get interested in anyone who forces his children to sign prenatal agreements.

8. Pretend to be royalty and you might mooch a free stallion season from a social climber or two.

7. On the way to the race, never play liar's poker with a bloodstock agent.

6. If somebody tries to sell you a raffle ticket for a Yugo, you're at the wrong party.

5. Don't invest in junk blonds.

4. Try to get dinner-table partners whose IQs exceed the numbers on their Jeep speedometers.

3. If your Derby date thinks Skye Terrace is the name of a horse, get another date.

2. Bet the favorite.

1. If you get bored, write your will and try to get somebody fired.

Monday, September 9, 1991

TO BUFFY, BEAUTY IS IN THE CREDIT CARD OF THE BEHOLDER

People are always asking me what Buffy Bleugrazz is wearing this season.

I really don't know. Buffy's closet is about the size of the Baltic republics.

But I saw our pseudonymous social arbiter this past weekend, and I asked her to describe her outfit.

"Well, I'm always willing to talk about clothes, darling," she said.

"Anything to relieve the boredom. You've heard of those persons who have near-death experiences? I'm waiting for a near-life experience."

Here's what Buffy said about her threads:

"Let's start at the top, darling. This thing on my head is a purple and green crested beret. The crest belongs to a prominent local country club that I was kicked out of after being temporarily engaged to a man the membership committee didn't like because he'd made a lot of money in a development deal and wouldn't cut any of them in on it."

She smiled sweetly.

"Moving along now, this is a trapeze jacket or swing jacket or whatever you want to call it. Underneath it is a purple, ribbed, 'poor boy' turtleneck sweater. And yes, I'm wearing enough Chanel rope chains to lynch a couple of horse thieves.

"Anyway, the jacket's lime green and matches my lime green miniskirt. Don't you just love them? I wrote a slightly cool check to buy them, but maybe the world will end before the banks open."

She sighed, took a sip of Vittelloise and tapped a sculpted nail on her tulip glass.

"Well, that's about it. Except for the quilted Chanel bag, the purple Norma Kamali tights, the suede gloves and the Ralph Lauren ankle boots.

"And yes, darling, I do need about a kilo of eyeliner and some pale lipstick. But that look won't fly with this face. It'll have to wait until my next lift."

"And yes, darling, all of my gold plastic is as soft as a first-grader's handful of gummi bears. My line of credit isn't even a line any more, it's more like a hyphen.

"And no, darling, it's not true that I've had cosmetic surgery everywhere. My navel is still the same.

"Anyway, I'm hoping there'll be somebody with money at the horse sales this month because I've had the most wonderful idea. I'm going to sell stock in myself. If Fasig-Tipton can do it, why can't I?"

"What kind of stock?" we asked.

"Preferred only," she said sharply. "I might be broke, darling, but I'm not common."

Sunday, March 15, 1992

SOCIAL COMMENT FROM BUFFY AND BARBARA JEAN

"What I want to know," said Barbara Jean, "is what are all those Secret Service agents protecting Bill Clinton from? The draft's over."

"Don't pay any attention to her, darling," said Buffy Bleugrazz, our pseudonymous social arbiter. "She's been watching far too much television."

"What I want to know," said Barbara Jean, "is after Tammy Faye Bakker gets divorced and starts dating again, what'll she say when some guy says, 'Tell me all about yourself?"

"Really, darling, who cares?" said Buffy.

"What I want to know," said Barbara Jean, "is why our tax dollars are going to be dumped into the campaign of some doofus running for governor of Kentucky? Why in the world are we giving working people's money to politicians?"

"She also watches KET, darling," said Buffy.

Barbara Jean is Buffy's rural cousin. I asked her what she thought about the economy.

"The depression's ending in my hometown of Duckville," she said. "I was there last weekend and saw three cars in a row with all four hubcaps. Plus the mayor just bought a new mobile home with his gold card."

"That's encouraging."

"It sure is, but what I want to know is how many checks do I have to bounce to get into the U.S. House of Representatives?"

"Some questions are unanswerable, darling," said Buffy. "That's what late winter is, you know — the season of unanswerable questions."

"Such as?" we asked.

"Oh, you know," said Buffy. "Which kind of hair conditioner should I try next? Is it time to worry about osteoporosis? How can I meet men who don't want to borrow my clothes?"

"Don't let her kid you," said Barbara Jean. "The only men she doesn't want to meet are in the cemetery."

"Do you two have any insights on what's chic this spring?" we asked.

"The accent will be on recovery, darling," Buffy said. "If your farm has been sold at auction and your spouse is in jail, don't mention it. Make happy talk."

"What I hate about this time of year is that it makes me feel so old," said Barbara Jean.

"How old are you?" we asked.

"Are you kidding?" said Barbara Jean. "I can remember when Calumet had money and Keeneland didn't sell T-shirts."

Wednesday, May 13, 1992

IS HIGH SOCIETY DEAD IN LEXINGTON?

We had heard that our pseudonymous social arbiter, Buffy Bleugrazz, had suffered a panic attack in her car.

"What happened?" we asked.

"It was terrible, darling," said Buffy. "I forgot my purse. What if I had been stranded on Man o' War Boulevard without my hormone pills?"

"That's not the real reason she panicked," said Barbara Jean, Buffy's rural cousin. "She's afraid that high society is dead in Lexington."

"Well, isn't it, darling?" said Buffy. "Now is the summer of our discontent. I might have to move away to Sadieville or Canada or somewhere."

"Why so?" we asked.

"My friends aren't the people in charge anymore, darling," said Buffy.

"They're all either in bankruptcy or Florida."

"Some of them are in both," said Barbara Jean.

"And some of them are so old, darling," said Buffy. "To know their true age, you'd have to cut off a leg and count the rings."

"But what about all the new people in Lexington?" we asked. "The ones who think they've made it into high society?"

"They haven't risen, darling," Buffy said. "Society has simply descended to where they are. Besides, they're the kind of people who eat catfish paté. They don't have the imagination to be true snobs."

"Then it's a failure of the imagination?"

"More than that," she said. "It's a failure of taste. And really, darling, one must have empathy, too. I truly admire anyone who can make it through life without a trust fund."

"I don't think that's empathy."

"Well, what's in a word, darling? The point is, people with money have an obligation to buy the best or the best will stop being made."

"Then it's a question of shopping?"

"Of course," said Buffy. "Life is one big shopping trip. We try on all kinds of things, don't we? Narcissism's not so bad if you don't take it personally."

Through all of this, we had noticed that Barbara Jean seemed profoundly bored. We asked why.

"Aw, I don't worry about that social stuff," Barbara Jean said. "I'm a Lexington intellectual."

"What's a Lexington intellectual?" we asked.

"Somebody who listens to National Public Radio all day," Barbara Jean said.

Sunday, July 19, 1992

BUFFY LONGS FOR GOLDEN, GLORIOUS DAYS OF GREED

"Remember the good old days?" said our pseudonymous social arbiter, Buffy Bleugrazz.

"Do you mean the days of wine and roses?" we asked.

"No, darling," she replied. "I mean the days of champagne and Arabs — Arabs in airplanes the size of Versailles. I mean the days when $700,000 was a stud fee, not an offer to buy your farm. I mean the days when you didn't have to serve KFC at your summer sales party. "

"Oh. Those days."

"It was the golden age of the horse business," Buffy said.

"How do you figure that?"

"Because all that mattered," she said, "was how much gold you had."

"But hasn't the horse business always been that way?"

"Perhaps it has, darling," Buffy said, "but it was better when it was more blatant. Things are so much nicer when people don't have to be ashamed of being greedy."

"As if any of your friends ever was ashamed of anything," said Barbara Jean, Buffy's rural cousin.

"It's not always their fault," Buffy said. "I knew a bloodstock agent once who tried to have a conscience implant, but his body kept rejecting it."

"He rejected it because the surgeons tried to put it next to his heart, but they couldn't find one," Barbara Jean said. "Anyway, you should have been here yesterday. I've never seen Buffy so upset."

"What happened?"

"Well, she'd gone shopping for plaid because plaid is going to be so big this fall. And some woman came up to her and said, 'I hope this doesn't offend you, but those sunglasses make you look just like Hillary Clinton.' Buffy took off one of her T-strap heels and tried to hit the woman with it."

"Really, darling," Buffy said, "she could have at least said Tipper Gore."

"Shoot," Barbara Jean said, "you ought to be happy she didn't say Barbara Bush."

"It made me feel like my next face lift will have to be on the rack at Quik Lube," Buffy said. "And please don't talk politics. What are any of those Washington politicians doing for the horse business? Don't they know Kentucky needs amoral rich people?"

"Speaking of politics," Barbara Jean said, "I think the vice-presidential race* is totally unfair to UK basketball fans. Who'd want to have to choose between Tennessee and Indiana?"

* In the 1992 presidential race, the vice-presidential candidates were Al Gore of Tennessee and Dan Quayle of Indiana.

Sunday, August 30, 1992

■ The BOPTROT scandal in the General Assembly, and the ensuing debate over ethics, caused the state universities to start requiring legislators to pay for their tickets to football and basketball GAMES — tickets they previously had gotten free.

OUR BUFFY IS TOO ETHICAL TO GIVE UP FREE UK TICKETS

"Would you give up free University of Kentucky basketball tickets for ethical reasons?" we asked Buffy Bleugrazz, our pseudonymous social arbiter.

"Are you crazy, darling?" said Buffy. "If I got free tickets, I'd have to accept them. It's a duty. The people of Kentucky want to see their socialite at the games. They want to see what she's wearing. A socialite has to fulfill her duties."

"You sound like the governor," we said.

"That's the great thing about Kentucky, darling," she said. "You can do almost anything and still be as ethical as the governor."

"Well, what do you think about the lieutenant governor making a show of paying for his UK tickets?"

"Oh, it's just a lot of hooey, darling. He's the biggest phony of all — there are 3 million other people in Kentucky who'd gladly pay for those same seats if they could get them. If he wanted to do something ethical, he could stop running for governor at the taxpayers' expense."

Barbara Jean, Buffy's rural cousin, glanced up from her book, a new paperback called *The FBI Killer*.

"I might be willing to give up my football tickets if I could still tailgate," Barbara Jean said.

"Be careful," we said. "What if the team goes 9-2 and gets a bowl game?"

"That'd be different," said Barbara Jean. "But nobody gives up basketball tickets. Shoot, there are people back home in Duckville who'd trade their mobile homes for seats behind the UK bench."

We asked Barbara Jean what she thought the bottom line was on this tickets-versus-ethics deal.

"Maybe the legislators ought to try letting some poor kids use those free tickets once in a while," she said. "Do you really think it matters whether a bunch of politicians come to the game?

"Have you ever heard a player say, 'Woe is me. I just can't get up to slam dunk today because the governor's not here.'

"Have you ever heard a fan say, 'Heck, let's go home. It's just not a game without half the General Assembly here.' "

We admitted that we had never heard anybody say those things.

"Well, then," she said, "maybe UK ought to give all the taxpayers a shot at tickets and distribute them by lottery every year."

"Darling!" said Buffy. "You're talking heresy. Do you have any idea of the money and kissing up that some people have expended to get The Right Seats?"

"You're right," said Barbara Jean. "Whatever was I thinking of? I almost stopped preaching and started meddling."

Sunday, February 14, 1993

EXPERIENCED COUSINS GIVE TIPS ON LOVE, DATING

Love was in the air, so we went to visit our pseudonymous social arbiter, Buffy Bleugrazz, and her rural cousin, Barbara Jean. They were sitting in the dark watching the UK-Notre Dame basketball game.

"Don't turn on the light, darling," Buffy said. "We look better this way."

"Our diets haven't kicked in yet," Barbara Jean said. "We're still covered with big blobs of fat. But we'll look great by April in time for the races."

"You two are women of some experience," we said.

"I'll say," Buffy said. "I can remember when life was fun and First Security was a bank."

"Heck," Barbara Jean said, "I can remember when life was fun and Kentucky Central was a big success."

"Well," we asked, "based on your experience with love and money, what helpful hints could you pass along for Valentine's Day?"

They both started talking at once. So here they are, Buffy's Rules of Love:

1. When you've seen all of a man's clothes, it's time for another man.

2. Men are like horses. They're only worth what someone will pay you for them.

3. A woman with money can always find a man, but a woman with a man can't always find money.

4. There is really no substitute for cash.

5. No matter what else he can do, if he can't get great Derby tickets, forget him.

And here they are, Barbara Jean's Principles of Dating:

1. Never date a man who looks through a whole bag of fried pork skins

trying to find the one with the little purple inspection stamp on it.

2. Never date a man who calls you because he saw your phone number spray-painted on an interstate highway bridge.

3. Never date a man who hangs around the public library because he can't afford to buy his own copy of Madonna's book.

4. Never date a younger man unless he's in the will.

5. Never date an older man unless you're in the will.

Saturday, October 7, 1995

BUFFY, BARB RACE TO BE IN FASHION AT THE TRACK

In a world of fleeting fads and fancies, some of life's great institutions are eternal. For instance, another October means another chance to lose your money at Keeneland Race Course.

The guy who started the place, Jack Keene, went broke building it. Some of the rest of us have gone broke maintaining it. And others have gone broke merely appearing at it.

"I need a sponsor for my hair," said Buffy Bleugrazz, our pseudonymous social arbiter.

"Fat chance," said her rural cousin, Barbara Jean. "Your hair costs more than some people's net income."

"But really, darling," Buffy said. "Wouldn't it be nice to see 'Buffy's Coif Courtesy of Sheik Abdullah' on one of those airplane banners that fly over the Keeneland backside?"

The two were discussing their outfits for opening day at the track.

"Guess what's back, darling," Buffy said. "Jackie O suit chic." For today's opener, she'll be wearing a tailored black St. John's knit with a matching black-and-white beret.

"Don't forget to say something about the accessories," Barbara Jean said.

"Buffy loves that little Gucci camera case bag with that little Gucci scarf tied to the handle. And those Ferragamo spike heels that look like something from The Rocky Horror Picture Show."

"Don't mind her, darling," Buffy said. "She's jealous. I happen to have a new Piaget wristwatch. The best she can do is a reconditioned Rolex."

It was true. But Barbara Jean does still have that Harry Winston pear-shaped diamond that her second husband gave her when he sold his strip mine in 1975.

"She loves to flash it around, darling, while she eats her burgoo," Buffy said.

For the fashion freaks in the audience, we asked Buffy to describe Barbara Jean's opening day outfit.

"Gladly, darling," Buffy said. "It's a Mondi ensemble. Yellow swing coat, black turtleneck, black-and-gold swing skirt with a snaffle-bit print and a snaffle-bit scarf. Just a little too self-conscious horsey, if you know what I mean."

"Is that all?"

"Not quite. She has a pair of over-the-knee black boots by either Charles David or the Marquis de Sade — you can't tell which. The black alligator shoulder bag is a Lana Marks, and it probably cost more than she'll ever have to put in it.

"Her black gloves aren't falling apart. They're supposed to look that way, darling. They're fringed. And she has one of those big 'Baywatch' haircuts, but hers is dyed red instead of blond.

"With all that black she's wearing and that ghastly pale lipstick outlined in taupe, all she needs is a sign around her neck that says: 'Visitation from 6 to 8 at the mortuary.'

"And oh, yes, darling — one other thing. She's wearing a pair of sunglasses that look like something John Gotti might have picked out."

"My, my," Barbara Jean said. "Aren't we feeling nasty today? Does it enhance your own tottering sense of self-esteem to criticize a sister socialite?"

"Socialite?" Buffy said. "Why, you weren't even a debutante."

"Maybe not," Barbara Jean said, "but I dated all their husbands."

The conversation seemed to be going downhill, sort of like the governor's race. We decided it was time to go.

Be sure to look for Buffy and Barbara Jean in the vicinity of the clubhouse today. They'll be the ones not speaking.

Tuesday, January 28, 1997

THE SKY'S THE LIMIT FOR SOCIALITES' NEXT TREND

Did you ever wonder: What will be the next big social trend in Lexington?

What will be the cultural tidal wave that will wash over the Manhattan of the Bluegrass and leave standing pools of fashionability all over the place?

We asked Buffy Bleugrazz, our pseudonymous social arbiter.

"Isn't it obvious, darling?" she said. "The sky box."

Good grief. We think she's got it.

"Just picture it," said Barbara Jean, Buffy's rural cousin. "There you are at a basketball game in some new or remodeled arena of the future, suspended high in the air above the Bubbas and Bubbettes far below."

"And yet," said Buffy, "as if by some subtle magic, you're not in the cheap seats. You're in the elite seats."

"Surrounded," said Barbara Jean, "by politicians, road contractors, old jocks, new CEOs and former distinguished state legislators out on parole."

"Can't you see it?" said Buffy. "Every social climber in 120 counties will want to be there. But of course, there won't be room for everyone, darling. That's the beauty of it."

"So," said Barbara Jean, "people who can't get in will start having their own sky boxes."

"Do you mean at home?" we asked.

"You bet," said Barbara Jean. "Right on top of their houses. And couples saying things to each other like: 'Well, the last time THEY had US over, it was in THEIR new sky box. How can we ask them over to OUR junky old patio? We'll just have to build a sky box.'"

"You're kidding," we said.

"We are not," Buffy said. "It'll be bigger than tailgating. And in a way that's what it is — tailgating for basketball. Best of all, having a sky box on top of your house will increase the value of your property."

We thought about it and it sounded right. We could imagine self-conscious neighbors competing to see who could build the biggest, most luxurious sky box.

This could be bigger than trying to have the most pretentious holiday lights and decorations. In Lexington, that's pretty big.

"And that's not all," said Barbara Jean. "There'll be sky boxes on mobile homes, too. Quick-fit aluminum in your choice of three colors — blue, white, and blue-and-white."

"Needless to say," said Buffy, "all this will trickle down to the younger generation."

"What she means," Barbara Jean said, "is there'll be whining kids saying stuff like: 'I wanna go play at Brittany's house 'cause she's got a Sky Box Barbie.'"

It was an appealing thought. Maybe there could be a Sky Box Ken, too, with a tiny glass of Wild Turkey in one of his little plastic hands.

People could start calling Lexington "Boxtown." Look at how "Beantown" has worked for Boston. Forget horse farms. We could have a box tour and a Kentucky State Box Park.

"Our top story tonight," we could hear a news anchor of the future droning: "Prisoners sue detention center to get sky box."

Actually, it is sort of cruel and unusual punishment not to have a chic seat.

Buffy says it'll no longer be fashionable when everybody has one. By then, it'll be out of hand.

We asked Barbara Jean how to know early on when this stuff has gone too far.

"Heck, that's easy," she said. "The first clue is when somebody dies and the funeral notice says: 'Services at the cemetery. Visitation before the game by invitation only in the sky box.'"

Tuesday, April 8, 1997

OUR BUFFY CHECKS OUT CHANGES AT THE TRACK

In Lexington, this is the way the old world ends.

Not with a bang or a whimper.

But with an announcer.

And a TV screen big enough to play handball on.

Last week, with the millennium drawing nigh, Keeneland Race Course closed its eyes, held its breath and bravely jumped into the 20th century.

"This is terrible, darling," said Buffy Bleugrazz, our pseudonymous social arbiter. "The place is turning into the Red Mile with higher prices."

"Aw, it's not so bad," said Barbara Jean, Buffy's rural cousin. "Between races, maybe the track can make a few pennies by using that new PA system to announce a blue-light special on T-shirts in the gift shop."

She glanced at some newly remodeled faces sitting together in one of the clubhouse dining rooms.

"There's enough plastic at that table to make a Corvette," said Barbara Jean.

Buffy was wearing a pale green St. John suit with off-white accents and a triple-strand pearl choker that looked as formidable as a set of brass knuckles.

She was dangling a quilted Chanel handbag by its gold chain, and her

T-strap shoes were by Patrick White.

Even her hair looked new. It was pared down and swept to one side.

Barbara Jean's curls were pulled back in a French twist. She had on a sky-blue, low-cut Armani suit and a couple of pounds of Bulgari jewelry.

She was clomping around on a pair of Stuart Weitzman platform shoes with lots of straps.

She was lugging her stuff in a Judith Leiber crocodile bag. Her eyes were concealed behind dark Paul Smith sunglasses. A Harry Winston diamond ring on one hand was bright enough to hurt your eyes.

The two of them looked like a couple of retro-'80s characters, but with a hint of '90s edginess.

They had arrived in Buffy's 10-year-old divorce-settlement Mercedes with a bumper sticker on it that said: "Ted Kennedy's Car Has Killed More People Than My Gun."

"Is she carrying concealed?" we asked Barbara Jean.

"Nothing but a trust fund check," said Barbara Jean. "She just put that sticker on her car to scare people. Buffy doesn't need a gun. She's tough enough to survive an autopsy."

The track this spring has more than the usual air of expectancy.

"At least the infield hasn't changed, darling," said Buffy. "I was afraid there might be a playground in it."

The idea of the racetrack as family entertainment would have sounded strange in the old days.

It would have been like trying to imagine some ancient railbird with Saratoga Restaurant gravy stains on his madras jacket looking down at a small child and saying:

"OK, kid, time for your vocabulary lesson. Can you say 'trifecta'?"

Different people see different Keenelands. What some natives thought was Tradition with a capital T, some visitors thought was provincialism, but not without its charm.

New York horse players used to come to Keeneland and say it still had the appeal of a "little country race course."

At the same time, some self-important Lexingtonians thought they soared above the common crowd by being in the clubhouse of the little country race course.

Not everyone is like that, of course. For those who are, perhaps the verticality is an illusion.

"Honey, that's the trouble with social climbing in the Bluegrass," Barbara Jean would say.

"Nobody wants to admit it's horizontal."

Tuesday, December 23, 1997

CELEBRATING THE HOLIDAYS IN STYLE

Maybe the best thing about the '90s in Lexington is that they're finally starting to look like the '80s.

The horse business is back.

Fur coats are back.

Our pseudonymous social arbiter, Buffy Bleugrazz, and her rural cousin, Barbara Jean, are back.

"New clothes and old jewelry are back, darling," said Buffy. "Even Christian Dior is back as a hot designer."

"Don't forget those Cats," said Barbara Jean. "We survived a coach transplant and Big Blue is back in the top five."

Buffy was wearing her blond hair straight and down over one eye. She had on smoky eye shadow and Chanel lipstick as red as Santa's suit.

Dangling from each side of her head was a pair of dazzling diamond drop earrings that she usually keeps in her lock-box at the bank.

"Floor length," Buffy said, "is back."

Buffy's holiday party outfit looked like it cost more than some people's whole Christmas.

She wore a red jersey floor-length tank dress by Mischka and an antique red-and-silver Chinese shawl with long fringe.

Some spare change was jangling in her Versace silver mesh bag. Her backless brocade shoes had stiletto heels so sharp that Barbara Jean looked at them and said:

"Honey, those things look like you could do heart surgery with them."

"That's exactly what I had in mind, darling," Buffy said. "I just haven't decided whose heart."

Barbara Jean laughed. "Buffy said she's going to find a new spouse this year — even if she has to go as far as Alaska."

Barbara Jean didn't look worried about anything. Her favorite expression is: "Thank God my second husband was a strip miner."

Her egg-shaped Cartier handbag probably had a wad of cash in it big enough to choke Cigar and one or two other horses.

At parties, Barbara Jean likes to get up close to your face and stare intently at you through her violet-tinted contact lenses. Then she asks her favorite question:

"Honey, who did your nose? It looks good."

She was wearing an enormous floor-length mink coat with chinchilla tuxedo trim and chinchilla cuffs.

Her Lacroix Couture party dress was a long black slip with lace trim at the hem, and her gold ankle-strap sandals were as scuffed as if she had just climbed a four-plank fence.

It turned out that she had scuffed them trying to kick in the door of her boyfriend's Lexus.

"He's now her former boyfriend," Buffy said. "I don't know what she caught him doing, but that's a terrible way to treat a pair of Fevrier shoes."

Barbara Jean changed the subject. She has an apocalyptic theory that Lexington is slowly sinking into the crumbly limestone beneath it.

"Don't you think that the buildings here look a little shorter every year?" she asked.

"Of course not," said Buffy. "They merely seem smaller because you've grown accustomed to them. When you arrived in Lexington, you thought the place was huge."

"They look a lot stubbier than they did when I moved here after the '74 coal boom," Barbara Jean insisted.

She added: "I bet the whole place will keep sinking until it's gone some-day. It'll be under the sea again, just like it was millions of years ago."

"Oh, that's absurd, darling," Buffy said with finality. "This place will never sink. It's too full of hot air."

CELEBS

Lexington is neither Hollywood nor New York, but it often plays host to the stars. Some arrive as guests for the Kentucky Derby; others are in town to perform. Some are in or near their prime; other have passed it. Either way, there's always something intriguing about the big names of the entertainment world. An earlier generation couldn't wait to dance to the music of rock 'n' roll pioneer Bo Diddley. Former child star Tom Kirk endured being asked, "Didn't you used to be somebody?" And then there was Zsa Zsa Gabor, who could not keep count of her husbands. Said the irrepressible actress: "A girl must marry for love and keep on marrying until she finds it."

Monday, July 8, 1985

BO DIDDLEY

"Back in 1955 . . . rock 'n' roll came alive . . ."
– Line from a Bo Diddley song

It was June 21, a sunny late afternoon in Lexington, and Elias McDaniel, 57, looked tired.

He had just flown in from his home in Hawthorne, Fla., a small town near Gainesville. He had about four hours to eat a steak-and-boiled-vegetable dinner from room service, take a shower, grab a nap and then go to work. The next day, he would catch a plane for Phoenix, Ariz.

Hardly anyone in the lobby noticed him as he stood at the Radisson Hotel registration desk, a stocky black man with heavily muscled arms and shoulders left over from a Golden Gloves boxing career 40 years ago.

He was wearing sunglasses, several pieces of turquoise jewelry, an open-neck sport shirt, dark trousers and cowboy boots. On his head was a large hat with a button that read "Blues Power."

Most of his luggage consisted of tall, flat, rectangular boxes — inside were electric guitar cases with faded stickers from all over the world: England, Australia, Germany, Switzerland, Canada.

The Radisson bell captain walked up and asked, in mixed tones of awe, admiration and curiosity: "Are you Bo Diddley?"

"Yeah, man," McDaniel said quietly. "I'm him." And he signed one more autograph.

Bo Diddley was there when rock 'n' roll began in July 1955. He helped it stay alive that year with a hit record, *Bo Diddley* with *I'm a Man* on the flip side, with a chunk-a-chunk-a-chunk-CHUNK-CHUNK guitar riff, a heavy, jungle-rhythm, blues-based beat with harmonic chording up and down the fingerboard that would later influence many rock performers, including Elvis Presley, the Beatles, the Rolling Stones, the Animals, the Yardbirds, the Doors and Bruce Springsteen.

"If I just had the money from my songs that were 'covered' (recorded by other artists)," he said, "I'd be a rich man today, you dig? Yeah, I'm a little angry."

McDaniel has been on the road 30 years, a living part of rock music history — from the early days when he played on several Chuck Berry recordings (including *Memphis* and *Sweet Little Rock 'n' Roller*), and had Top 20 records of his own (*Say Man* and *You Can't Judge a Book by the Cover*) to the early 1960s when he was ludicrously "packaged" for a white, teen-age market with an album called *Surfin' with Bo Diddley* to the late '60s when his songs were repopularized by British groups to the early '70s when he was "rediscovered" in the wave of 1950s nostalgia to the late '70s when he was the opening act for the Clash on their 1979 U.S. tour to the '80s when he continues to play one-nighters and does an occasional film spot, making cameo appearances in the Eddie Murphy-Dan Aykroyd movie *Trading Places* and the George Thorogood video, *Bad to the Bone*.

And listening to McDaniel talk about the 1950s is like hearing Bo Diddley singing the rock 'n' roll blues — a sort of flip side to *Happy Days*.

"Those sharp cats in the record companies," he said, "they made the money off people like me. Chuck Berry was more hep — he made some money. I didn't have the education to know what was happening.

"I figure Chess Records (a Chicago company that recorded him in the early years) owes me $3 million, maybe $4 million. But who knows, man? It's all so complicated. Lawyers, lawyers, lawyers. They go through bankruptcy, they go through reorganization.

"In all those years my songs were on the radio, I don't believe they made me $50,000, I swear. This jive is still happenin', you dig? A kid come up to me last year and says: 'I had a No. 1 record for 11 weeks — and the record company say I owe them $10,000 — How can that be?' Funky, huh? Yeah. But you try to do anything about it back then, the record companies would shut you down, tell the radio stations to stop playin' your records.

"Like when I was tourin' back then. The promoter says, 'Why ain't you playin' one more hour? I'm payin' you $1,500 – I want my money's worth.' And I say: 'What's this $1,500 talk? You only payin' $1,200.' The agent got it, you dig? He puts $300 in his own pocket and tells me it's a $1,200 gig. Then he take 10 percent of that $1,200, too."

McDaniel held up a cassette titled *Ain't It Good to Be Free*. "This is my new one," he said. "And I mean mine. I got my own record company now; sell it mail-order from my home in Hawthorne, Fla. It's cool. But maybe they try to shut me down again. Then it ain't cool."

He was born Elias Bates in 1928 on a farm near McComb, a small town in southern Mississippi. An orphan, he was adopted by a sharecropper family named McDaniel.

When he was 5, the family migrated to Chicago, where he grew up on the south side of the city, his life an amalgam of contrasting musical influences — the classical violin lessons he had in childhood, the swelling, hymnal tones of the big organ in the Ebenezer Baptist Church to which his mother took him, the Mississippi Delta blues recordings of Muddy Waters and

John Lee Hooker.

By his early teen-age years, he was playing guitar on street corners for tips and boxing as a light heavyweight in a Chicago gym, where he got the Bo Diddley nickname that later became his stage name.

"I was a pug," he said, "a bo diddley. That's street talk for 'tough guy.' I quit school when I was 16; my mother was sickly. I got a job, grocery delivery. Hey, $18 a week. That was a lot of money in the ghetto back then."

By 1951, he was playing the 708 Club in Chicago, and became an established rhythm-and-blues performer over the next four years. In July 1955, he signed his first record contract, the same month that Bill Haley's *Rock Around the Clock* zoomed onto national song charts and launched the rock 'n' roll era.

"Rock 'n' roll," sighed McDaniel as he sat in his room at the Radisson 30 years later. "Yeah. Let me tell you about that. It was funky back then. There was this stupid racial thing. If you did your fine song and you were black, they called it R&B (rhythm and blues). If you did the same song and you were white, they called it rock 'n' roll.

"What happened, see, was that white kids started digging this R&B music on the radio and they wanted to buy those records. But their parents, they said, 'This isn't proper music for you. Don't you buy those records.'

"So white artists 'covered' those records, but they couldn't call their material R&B, because R&B was black people's music. So Alan Freed (a white New York radio disc jockey) called it rock 'n' roll.

"Alan used to play my records and say: 'Here's a man with an original sound — it'll rock you back in your seat and roll you on the floor!'

"Yeah. I had studied classical violin. I knew things about music; I knew what words like glissando and diminuendo meant. My guitar had an organ-like sound.

"You know the only dude that had done anything real rhythmical on the guitar up till then? Gene Autry, believe it or not.

"You know why rock 'n' roll's still here? 'Cause it came from the blues. And all people can understand the blues. Black people, white people. A poor man gets the blues, but so does a rich man. Everybody gets the blues. Now I'm gonna have dinner."

He scooted his chair over to the room-service tray and flipped through the channels on the hotel television. For a second he watched a Home Box Office video, a sadistic parody of 1950s rock 'n' roll with a song that went:

"Everybody run — the homecoming queen's got a gun . . ." Then he turned the dial to an old segment of *Little House on the Prairie* and settled down to eat.

Four hours later, McDaniel was playing with four local pickup musicians at a private party at the Lafayette Club. There was an odd incongruity to the scene. His guitar speakers were propped up on two of the club's salmon-colored, herringbone-patterned armchairs; hanging on the wall in the background were handsomely framed fox-hunting prints.

"Bo Diddley, Bo Diddley, where you been?" he sang. " 'Round the world and back again."

A young woman in the crowd looked at nobody in particular and asked: "Who's Bo Diddley?"

Friday, June 20, 1986

DONALD O'CONNOR

Dancing? I've done it all my life. I can't jump as high, but I'm still shifty. What I could never do now is compete with people's memories of me.
— Donald O'Connor

Along with Gene Kelly and Debbie Reynolds, he was a star in *Singin' in the Rain* in 1952. It may have been the greatest Hollywood musical ever made.

Millions of people still watch it each year on television.

There was no rain falling in Ballroom No. 4 of the Radisson Plaza Hotel just after noon yesterday, but Donald O'Connor's face was cloudy. He was ready to rehearse, and the piano player wasn't there yet.

"This is gonna make my life miserable," he said.

A woman stopped by to say: "We're taking your golf clubs on out to the course, Mr. O'Connor."

"Thank you, dear lady," O'Connor said.

He glanced over at Robert Morse, the Broadway entertainer best remembered as the star of a hit show called *How to Succeed in Business Without Really Trying*. "Are we gonna play together, Bobby?" he asked.

"Whatever happens," Morse replied.

O'Connor, Morse and several other Hollywood-type celebrities — including actors Hal Linden and Dale Robertson — are in town for the Children's Charity Golf Classic slated for Saturday at Greenbrier Country Club. They do some entertaining, and locals bid money for the privilege of playing golf with them; last year, the event raised $112,000 for nine child-related charities.

"Let's do something, Sid," O'Connor said to his performing partner, Sidney Miller. The two sat down at the piano; Miller played and both sang. "Sid and I have been working together since 1942," O'Connor said. "But I first met Sidney in ... oh, 1933 or '32. I was playing the Orpheum Theatre in Los Angeles. Sid and Mickey Rooney were great friends; they came on stage and did their famous slow-motion wrestling routine. And that's how I met Sidney."

O'Connor got up to walk off some nervous energy. He stepped easily onto a narrow stage in the center of the ballroom, much lighter on his feet than most 60-year-old men. His feet began tapping; he crossed a leg, gave it a rhythmical slap and smiled. For a second, he resembled the pert-faced vaudeville hoofer that he played in so many movies.

It was type-casting. O'Connor grew up in a vaudeville family. "There were six of us," he said. "The O'Connor Family — that was the act. We worked very, very hard. We had a lot of fun."

The night before, O'Connor had had dinner at the Merrick Inn. At his table were Hal Linden, the star of TV's *Barney Miller* and *Blacke's Magic*, and two local residents: horsewoman Anita Madden, who is a longtime friend of O'Connor and his wife, Gloria, and Mary Margaret Lochmueller, one of the organizers of the Children's Charity Golf Classic.

"(Gene) Kelly doesn't dance anymore," O'Connor had said. "He can't do the lifts. And Astaire is past 80. Fred was always so light on his feet that he looks like he's dancing when he's sitting down. And me. I still dance a little, you see. Only a little."

He had reminisced about his vaudeville days. "I remember once we played Louisville," he said. "The electricity went off in the middle of the show. There was a flood. We turned on flashlights and went on with the jokes. When we didn't hear any laughter, we pointed the flashlights at the audience — and no one was there. Suddenly we noticed a peculiar sensation about our ankles. It was water."

He was asked about *Singin' in the Rain*. At the time he was making the film, had he realized that it would turn out to be such a classic?

"We knew it was going to be a good picture," he said. "All the departments in the studio cooperated wonderfully. When that happens, there's a magic to what you do."

Meanwhile, back at the Radisson yesterday afternoon, the piano player had finally arrived. However, in one of those mysteries whose solution is known only to those in show business, O'Connor left 10 minutes later on his way to the golf course. "See you tonight, dear boy," he sang on his way out the door.

There was a feeling of backstage tension in the air. It might have had something to do with the music. Not one of the three — O'Connor, Miller and Morris — had appeared pleased with the partial run-throughs.

Ms. Lochmueller, who was helping coordinate the rehearsal and trying to keep all the egos soothed, looked as if she wouldn't mind taking a tranquilizer. "I just keep telling myself to keep smiling," she said.

It brought to mind that producing a show — any show, even a charity show — is a hard job to take on.

Earlier O'Connor had said, "They tell me I began dancing at 13 months of age."

Thirteen months?

"Oh, yes,' he said. "I'm serious."

After 59 years in show business, he probably didn't need a rehearsal anyway.

Sunday, May 24, 1987

CLAYTON MOORE, THE LONE RANGER

GEORGETOWN — Somebody once said that the true test of an intellectual is to be able to listen to the William Tell Overture without thinking of the Lone Ranger.

Everybody at the grand opening of Indian Acres Shopping Center in Georgetown yesterday would have flunked the test, and no wonder — there was the Lone Ranger in person, 72-year-old actor Clayton Moore.

"Hi, little kids! Hi, big kids! Have you had your Cheerios this morning?" he said as he ascended a flat-bed trailer decorated with bales of straw and a saddle while the William Tell Overture played on a public address system.

Naturally, he was wearing his black mask. "I only take it off to wash my face," he quipped.

Moore also was wearing a blue cowboy suit, a white hat and a red neckerchief. He looked like a combination of nostalgia item and a U.S. flag.

But he did not arrive on Silver, the white horse he rode on the old ABC-TV series that ran from 1949 to 1956. He arrived in a white Chrysler limousine.

Moore gets several thousand dollars for a personal appearance, and the deal always includes first-class travel.

On Friday night, at a reception in his honor at Spindletop Hall in

Fayette County, he had talked about his Hollywood career during an interview. Moore is a Chicago native who had been a male model in New York before going to Hollywood in 1938.

"I got my Western education at Republic Studio," he said. "It was a great place to be — John Wayne was there, too."

In the 1940s, Moore starred in dozens of "B" pictures, as low-budget films are called, including serials with titles like The Perils of Nyoka.

"Nobody made more Saturday morning serials than I did, even Buster Crabbe," he said. "But I'm the original Lone Ranger, the original — I made 169 TV shows and two feature-length motion pictures. I am the Lone Ranger."

His blue eyes did not blink when he said that. In fact, he looked somewhat obsessed. What does he mean when he says he is the Lone Ranger?

"I mean I feel that Clayton Moore and the Lone Ranger are one and the same," he said. "I believe in my country, my fellow man and my creator. There's no other country like America. Where else could some poor kid have the opportunity to one day grow up and serve as U.S. president?"

Moore said he's had "dozens of offers to return to acting" but "I won't do it, I won't play other roles. I'm the Lone Ranger and that's it."

Tonto, his Indian sidekick and "kemo sabe" (which means "faithful friend," said Moore), was played by actor Jay Silverheels, who died in 1980 and never took the TV imagery quite that seriously.

Silverheels, who used to race harness horses at The Red Mile in Lexington back in the 1970s, once was asked why he didn't race Scout, his horse on the TV show. "Heck," he replied, "I could beat Scout."

But of course, no one can beat the Lone Ranger and his silver bullets. Even the company that owns the Lone Ranger trademark found that out a few years ago when Moore said he fought for in court — and won — the right to wear the black mask instead of sunglasses at his shopping center appearances.

"I'd like to go on doing this for another 72 years," said Clayton Moore. Hi-yo, Silver, away!

Friday, May 6, 1988

ZSA ZSA GABOR

Imagine a blond, green-eyed, rapid-talking, Hungarian-accented tornado in a Russian lynx coat — "I hope it's a good one, darling, it was 150,000 bucks" — carrying a black Shih Tzu puppy, followed by bottles of Moet & Chandon Brut Imperial champagne and a mountain of Vuitton luggage in a procession of two limousines and one van from Blue Grass Airport to the Hyatt Regency Hotel.

Imagine all that, my dear, and you have the way that Zsa Zsa Gabor arrived in Lexington yesterday afternoon.

Her eighth husband, Prince Frederick von Anhalt, Duke of Saxony and, his wife says, heir to the German throne, if there were still a German throne, couldn't make it.

"He has a cold, my dear," said Gabor, "and he is finishing a $20 million deal with the Germans and Chinese — something to do with manure, I think — Eureka, is that the word?"

"Fertilizer," said her personal secretary, Brian DeShazor, leaning over the front seat of the limo. "Eureka Fertilizer."

"Yes, fertilizer," said Gabor. "That's a nicer word."

She has been described as one of the world's true celebrities — someone who is famous for being famous.

"Zsa Zsa is kind to all of her husbands," quipped Hermen Greenberg, whose wife, Monica, was sitting next to Gabor in the limo. "She always gives them back their rings and keeps the stones."

"That's a joke, darling," she said. "All of my husbands cost me money. I don't know anything about sex — I was always married. A girl must marry for love and keep on marrying until she finds it.

"When (hotel magnate) Conrad Hilton and I parted, Conrad was very generous. He gave me five million — five million Gideon Bibles."

The Greenbergs, of Washington, D.C., on whose chartered plane Gabor arrived, are her friends. She will be going with them to the Kentucky Oaks today, to Preston and Anita Madden's Derby party tonight and to the Kentucky Derby on Saturday.

She loves to talk about her Tennessee walking horse, Silver Fox, and her line of cosmetics from Zsa Zsa Ltd. "My mother says I should tell people I'm 70. 'Tell them you're older than you are — you'll sell more face cream,' she says."

She was asked if it was true that she once offered $10,000 to anyone who could prove she'd had cosmetic surgery.

"It was $1 million, darling," she said. "It was always $1 million. I don't need surgery; my face gets so much exercise from talking all the time."

She mentioned her forthcoming book, *One Lifetime Is Not Enough*. "We've had one $5 million offer, but we're putting it on the auction block. I tell everything in the book — all about my seven husbands whose names I can't remember. It will be a second *Dynasty*, like on television."

She lives in Los Angeles, in Bel Air, "in the Howard Hughes house, next door to Nancy Reagan's new house, with three horses, one cat and five dogs.

"That is why I have the prince, to clean the rug when the dogs misbehave — no, I'm joking, darling; I clean the rug.

"I'm never jealous, only when I have a man. If I catch someone looking at my man, I shoot them."

The two-limo-one-van procession pulled up in front of the Hyatt. The lobby was crowded with women carrying shopping bags.

It was a convention. A large sign read: WELCOME KENTUCKY EXTENSION HOMEMAKERS.

Gabor was instantly recognized. Several of the women rushed forward, asking for autographs and popping flashcubes as they snapped photos.

One of the conventioneers, Martha Claycomb of Brandenburg, a woman with red hair, was delighted with the autograph she received on a scrap of paper. It simply read: "Zsa Zsa."

Gabor usually signs that way. If she signed her full name, it would be quite an autograph: Zsa Zsa Gabor Belge Hilton Sanders Cosden Hutner Ryan O'Hara von Anhalt.

"She's a super nice personality," said Ms. Claycomb. "Not like some celebrities who brush you off. She told me she likes redheads, that she used to be a redhead and they turned her blond for Hollywood."

Sunday, May 8, 1988

ZSA ZSA GABOR GETS HER MINT JULEP — AND MORE

"I want a mint julep," said Zsa Zsa Gabor. "I've never had a mint julep." She didn't get it.

It was noon yesterday, take-off time for the helicopter to leave the Hamburg Place polo field and fly to Louisville, where Gabor was scheduled to present the winner's trophy in the fourth race at Churchill Downs.

A few minutes later, she was 1,000 feet in the air over the undulating green landscape of the Bluegrass, working on her makeup.

"I'm petrified of helicopters, darling," she said. "I've only flown in one before this, when Mr. (Chuck) Yeager took me on a ride at Las Vegas. Do you know him? He's the one who broke the sound barrier."

She talked about men. "When I was a baby, I am told, whenever a woman would approach my crib, I would scream. Whenever a man approached, I would coo and giggle."

She showed two wallet snapshots that she always carries with her.

They were faded, black-and-white photographs of her and the late actor George Sanders, her third husband, who committed suicide in 1972, leaving behind a note that said he had seen all of life and was bored with it.

"He was my great love," she said. "I adored him completely. He was a difficult man."

By the time the helicopter touched down at Louisville, she had enjoyed the ride. "How much would this helicopter cost?" she asked pilot Scott Runyan.

"About $500,000," he said.

"I want it," she said. "Would you like to work for me?"

Runyan laughed.

"I want a mint julep," she said, as a van took her and horseman Preston Madden, her host, to a waiting limousine with a police escort.

She didn't get it.

She forgot about the julep the second she spotted a souvenir stand. The limo and police cruiser had to wait while she went shopping.

She bought Derby sweatshirts, key chains, sets of drinking glasses, sun visors — a pile of merchandise in a few moments.

"That'll be $174.90," said the vendor.

She had her money out when Madden stepped up, said, "Allow me," and placed two $100 bills in the vendor's hand.

"You are the first man who ever gave me back my money," Gabor told him, smiling and batting her eyelashes.

"I'm just glad you weren't standing at Tiffany's," said Madden.

Fifteen minutes later, the limo arrived at the Downs.

"I want a mint julep," she said.

She didn't get it. She stopped to shop for Derby T-shirts instead.

Finally, just before the fourth race, she made it to the President's Room of the Downs clubhouse.

"I want a mint julep," she said. She got it. She stood on a balcony and took one sip as the crowd below screamed up at her: "Hey, Zsa Zsa, baby!"

Then she dashed off to present the race trophy.

When she returned, she put the julep aside. "Only one tiny drink, sweetheart, is all I can take. Now I want a no-calorie Coca-Cola."

"Zsa Zsa," everyone kept asking her, "who are you betting on in the Derby?"

"The filly, darling," she said. "I want a winner."
She got it.

Friday, May 5, 1989

TERRY MOORE, ACTRESS

She left Los Angeles at 11 o'clock Wednesday night.

But when Hollywood actress Terry Moore — blond hair, blue eyes and seductive smile floating above a bosomy fox jacket — popped off the plane at Blue Grass Airport at 9:30 a.m. yesterday, she was as fresh as a peppermint.

She joked about Burt Reynolds.

"He's so cute. The only person I want to be tonight is Loni Anderson. And tomorrow night, too. Let me tell you, his wedding was the only one I ever cried over."

She talked about her new TV talk show, *Terry's World*, which is being bid for syndication. "I even got John Travolta," she said. "Barbara Walters never got him."

By the time she was having lunch at the Coach House Restaurant, she was up on the floor demonstrating a rah-rah routine from her cheerleading days at Glendale High School.

Moore, who co-stars with Martin Sheen in *Beverly Hills Brats*, a new United Artists movie to be released in August, is one of the early arrivals for Derby Weekend.

"It's the first time I've played a parent," she said of the movie.

"Martin plays my husband — a Beverly Hills plastic surgeon with a license plate on his car that says NIP-N-TUCK."

Moore was famous for her sexy movie roles of the 1950s. She was in some of the best-known films — such as *Peyton Place* — that defined the era.

And she was nominated for an Oscar for her performance in *Come Back, Little Sheba*.

But it was her off-screen love life that generated the biggest headlines, especially a romance with billionaire Howard Hughes.

Years later, Hughes' death brought her additional publicity. She sued the Hughes estate as his widow.

She and Hughes had been secretly married when she was 18, she said, in a ceremony performed by the captain of Hughes' yacht off the coast of Mexico — and they had never been legally divorced.

The news media went wild with that one. The Hughes estate settled the case out of court, Moore wrote a book about the whole thing called *The Beauty and the Billionaire* and then — incredibly, at age 55 — she posed for a nude photo spread in *Playboy* magazine.

"I did that to prove a point," she said. "In Hollywood, they think you're over the hill at 25."

Now, five years later, one of her projects is putting together a movie based on her book.

"Sean Connery wants to play Howard," she said.

And who'll play her?

"Madonna's agent called me," she said, "but I think Madonna's too old for the part. We'll need an actress who's about 16."

Moore will be at Preston and Anita Madden's Derby Eve party at Hamburg Place tonight and go to the Derby on Saturday on the luxury bus of Hilary Boone's Wimbledon Farm.

And wherever else she is this weekend, we can promise you one thing.

It won't be dull.

Friday, November 2, 1990

TOMMY KIRK, CHILD STAR GROWN UP

"How do people react when they meet you?" he was asked.

"Sometimes they're shocked," said Tom Kirk, 48. "They say, 'Didn't you used to be somebody?'

"Once I was walking down Wilshire Boulevard, and there were these two girls. I heard one say to the other: 'He looks like somebody from the '50s.'"

Somebody from the '50s.

Thirty years ago, he was Tommy Kirk, and he was a movie star. He starred in some of the most profitable Walt Disney movies ever made: *Old Yeller, The Shaggy Dog, The Absent-Minded Professor, Swiss Family Robinson, Son of Flubber, The Monkey's Uncle.*

"I saw Mr. Disney at a party once — the only time I ever saw him socially outside the studio — and he called me his 'good luck charm.'

"I made a lot of money, and I spent it all," Kirk said. "No bitterness, no regrets. I did what I did."

Kirk was a teen-ager earning $1,000 a week more than 30 years ago. Today that would be about like making $5,000 a week.

"I was young and dumb," he said. "And then I was broke."

Kirk, who is visiting Lexington, rode a bus here from Los Angeles. He has been a waiter, a chauffeur, and today he cleans carpets for a living.

"It's my own one-man business," he said of the carpet cleaning.

Kirk was born in Louisville. "My dad worked for the highway department, just a temporary kind of job. My mom was a stenographer. We went west — my folks, my older brother, Joe, and I — during the World War II years."

His father found a job at an aircraft company.

"Joe was star struck," Kirk said. "He was 16, and I was 12 when he tried out for a production of Eugene O'Neill's *Ah, Wilderness* at Pasadena Playhouse.

He said, 'Why don't you try out, too? There's a part for a kid.'

"Well, it had five lines, it didn't pay anything, and nobody else showed up, so I got the part. A Hollywood agent saw me in the play, called my parents and asked to represent me."

His brother later became a dentist. But by the time Kirk was 14, he was playing one of the Hardy boys in films shown on the old Mickey Mouse Club TV show.

When he was 18, he made five movies back to back. He had spent his youth working. His friends were other actors, such as Annette Funicello and Kevin Corcoran.

"Annette's a millionaire, but try to get her to lend you $5," Kirk said, laughing. "And Kevin's a disgustingly successful producer. And I'm disgustingly poor."

He was 22 when Disney fired him from a seven-year contract. Kirk will not say why, but he does say:

"I wasn't the 'boy next door' anymore. I could pretend to be for a few hours a day in front of the camera. But I couldn't live it. I'm human. I'm not St. Francis of Assisi.

"At Disney, you had to meet the 'family image' or you were out. I knew the rules, and I broke them. I'm not crying about it."

After that, he said, came a "downward spiral of 'B' movies" with titles such as: *The Ghost in the Invisible Bikini, Mars Needs Women, Mother Goose a' Go-Go* and *It's Alive,* which Kirk says was "a monster movie so cheap that the monster wore a scuba suit and had ping-pong balls for eyes."

Kirk was enjoying his Kentucky visit this week. He has written a script about Abraham Lincoln that he hopes will one day be produced.

On Tuesday night, at a house on Davidson Court, Kirk handed out candy to trick-or-treaters.

Not one of them recognized the pleasant, witty, middle-aged man as someone who once was famous.

There was a time when just about every kid in America would have known him.

But that was long ago, and this was a Disney story with a different kind of endings.

Tommy Kirk, who as a child star made so many successful movies for Walt Disney, was fired by the studio when it became known that he was gay.

Tuesday, April 29, 1997

HAS-BEENS AND WANNABES — THE STUFF DERBY IS MADE OF

Once upon a time, not so many years ago, a beautiful, blond young woman came to the Kentucky Derby. She was a guest from Hollywood, and there are few easier things in life than to be a celebrity guest in the Bluegrass at Derby time.

A limousine with champagne meets you at the airport. Somebody else carries the designer luggage and somebody else takes care of the hotel room.

In fact, somebody else takes care of everything. All you have to do is show up and smile.

She danced at the Madden Derby Eve bash. On Derby Day, she rode to Churchill Downs on a VIP luxury bus that was like a rolling party with its own bartender and white-jacketed servers.

She sat in a box at Churchill Downs. Because she had a role in a popular situation comedy, a lot of people recognized her from TV.

Photographers took her picture. People stared at her, some frankly and some sideways from under their Derby hats while pretending not to look.

Two little girls dressed up for the track in Laura Ashley clothes shyly asked her for an autograph.

When she signed their race programs, they giggled and ran back to their parents in triumph.

The little girls had looked happier than she did. She wondered aloud how long there would be fans, how long the TV show would last.

The star of the show was a silver-haired veteran actor with a booming voice and a famous face. She played one of his daughters who lived in an upstairs apartment over their father's house.

The star had been in show business for 30 years before he finally landed a role in a TV show that had been a huge hit and made him famous.

She said she felt as if she hadn't paid her dues. That was why she worried that it was all a bubble that would soon burst.

She had acted in college productions in Colorado, where she was on the school ski team. She had gone to Hollywood, and a casting director picked her for the TV show at her first audition.

People in Hollywood told her she was unbelievably lucky. It was once in a lifetime. It would never happen again.

After working there a while, she saw what they meant. It would be incredibly difficult to repeat her first success.

She wondered if she should get married instead. Her father was in government service. She had grown up in a traditional family, not a Hollywood family.

Her Derby escort was a handsome young man from Kentucky who was in the clothing business in Los Angeles. She said he was just a friend.

But it was hard to find a Hollywood actor worth marrying, she said. Behind the glamour was a lot of self-absorbed misery.

The Monday after the Derby, she got on a plane and flew back to Los Angeles.

Later I heard she got engaged to the man from Kentucky, but it didn't work out. He married someone else.

And after that, I heard she had a baby and was trying to write instead of act.

Her name was Lydia Cornell. She was on a TV show called *Too Close For Comfort*.

The silver-haired star of the show was Ted Knight, famous as the hammy news anchor on *The Mary Tyler Moore Show*. He died in 1986.

After *Too Close For Comfort* went off the air, I never saw her on TV again or at the Derby again.

There are a lot of stories like that this time of year, stories of fleeting fame and races past.

Saturday, May 2, 1998

BUDD SCHULBERG, AUTHOR

It seems like all my friends are on postage stamps.
— Budd Schulberg, 84

There are Hollywood celebrities and then there are Hollywood legends.

One face in the Kentucky Derby crowd today is legendary Hollywood writer and Academy Award winner Budd Schulberg, a guest at the Madden Derby Eve party last night.

"I've always wanted to come to the Derby," he said yesterday before buying a magnifying glass at the Radisson Hotel so he could read the small print in *The Racing Form.*

"Gene Markey used to invite me many years ago, but I didn't make it until now." (Markey was a husband of Lucille Markey, a former owner of Calumet Farm.)

Classic-film buffs probably best know Schulberg's work from an Academy Award best picture winner called *On the Waterfront* (1954).

In a scene in the back seat of a car — a scene that became a classic in American film — Marlon Brando, playing a heartbroken, washed-up boxer, says to Rod Steiger, playing his ruthless brother who exploited his career: "Charlie, Charlie ... I coulda been a contender, Charlie. ... I coulda been a contender instead of a bum ..."

Schulberg won an Oscar for that screenplay.

When he tells his stories about other writers now on postage stamps, the literary giants who were his friends — F. Scott Fitzgerald, Ernest Hemingway, Sinclair Lewis — Schulberg doesn't just tell them.

He relives them, sometimes with tears in his eyes. It's easy to see the emotion, the heart that drives his writing.

"It was despicable the way Scott (Fitzgerald) was treated in Hollywood," he said. "His producers knew he needed money desperately and they never paid him what he was worth."

Asked what Fitzgerald, who died in 1940 nearly broke and with all of his books out of print, would be writing about if he were alive in 1998, Schulberg said: "I'm not sure, but the biggest difference is that Scott, who wrote so much about the rich, would be a millionaire himself in today's market. He would finally be the rich."

Schulberg, a Dartmouth College graduate, grew up in Hollywood, where his father, B.P. Schulberg, was a Paramount producer.

Budd Schulberg wrote a best-selling, then-shocking novel about the cut-throat nature of the movie business when he was 26.

It was called *What Makes Sammy Run?* His father begged him not to publish it.

"He said it would damage not only me, but our whole family, for we were a Hollywood family," Schulberg recalled. "And after it was published, Louis B. Mayer of MGM (Metro-Goldwyn-Mayer), the 'godfather' of Hollywood, called me 'a traitor' and seriously wanted me to be deported from the United States."

A Hollywood movie was never made of that book, but Schulberg said: "It still might happen all these years later. There's a project under way where I get a year to do the screenplay, but I can't really talk about it yet."

For his Derby pick yesterday, Schulberg was leaning a little toward Cape Town, but was far from making up his mind.

Like a true horse player, he planned to be at Churchill Downs in time for the first race of the day.

"Budd is good at picking them," said his wife, Betsy Schulberg.

But she did have one complaint about her writing husband: "I can't get him to sign all my copies of his books."

FAMOUS KENTUCKIANS

To residents of the Bluegrass State, it is an honor just to be a Kentuckian. How much greater then to be, or have been, a famous Kentuckian — such as politician A.B. "Happy" Chandler, businessman and thoroughbred breeder C.V. "Sonny" Whitney, broadcaster Nick Clooney or the world-famous icon for fried chicken, Harland Sanders. Each of them represents something distinctive about the success enjoyed by the most memorable Kentuckians. Together, they represent what makes Kentucky a colorful and proud state.

Wednesday, October 3, 1984

'HAPPY' LEFT OFF QUEEN'S GUEST LIST, BUT NOT LEFT SPEECHLESS

From the Department of Woodford County Wallflower:

We had heard a rumor that 86-year-old former Gov. A.B. "Happy" Chandler had been left off the guest list for Queen Elizabeth II, who will be staying at millionaire Texan Will Farish's Lane's End Farm in Woodford County, just a hoot and a holler from Chandler's home in Versailles.

Sure enough, Chandler, who first met the queen when she was a freckle-faced kid, was willing to say a few hundred words about the snub, royalty he has known, World War II, married life, baseball, etc.:

"Well, I didn't expect to be invited. There are new fellows here now, from Texas and other places. And my father told me once: "Never go anyplace where you're not invited."

"But let me say, pardner, I wonder if there's any other Kentuckian who goes as far back with the royal family as I do. Now, Mama (his wife, Mildred Chandler) and I met King Edward VIII after he abdicated the throne to marry Wallis Simpson. We met him at a party in Florida. After he abdicated, you know, he was the governor general of the Bahamas.

"And I met King George VI at Buckingham Palace in England in 1943. That's probably a little before your time, World War II. Well, I was one of five members of the Senate Committee on Military Affairs that toured world battlefields. We flew across the Indian Ocean from Ceylon to Australia, too.

"I met King George at Buckingham Palace and his two little girls, Elizabeth and (Princess) Margaret, who were just little tykes, you understand, playing around the palace grounds. Well, King George autographed a 'short snorter' for me. Now, you might not know what that is. Well, a short snorter is a Confederate bill. I've still got his autograph on it.

"Winston Churchill autographed one for me, too. And of course, I knew Lady Astor. She told me once that Churchill didn't like her for two reasons — she was an American and she was a woman. She was a Virginia girl, pardner. She's the one who told Churchill: 'Winston, if I were your wife, I'd give you arsenic.' And he told her: 'Lady Astor, if I were your husband, I'd take it.'

"And I remember when they dedicated the St. Lawrence Seaway in 1957, I was at a luncheon with the queen and Prince Philip in Chicago. But I've got no complaints, my friend. Every day's a good day; some are just better than others.

"Mama and I'll be married 60 years next November (1985). How about that? And Mama's just fine. Somebody told me once: 'I hear your wife is outspoken.' And I said: 'By whom?'

"Once I didn't speak to Mama for three weeks — I didn't want to interrupt her. And did I ever tell you about the time that Mama wanted me to take her someplace that she'd never been? So I took her to the kitchen.

"I guess I've met all the famous people of my time. Anyway, I think I'm going to the World Series this year, so I might not be here next week. They invite me every year, you know.

"And I'll be wearing my (University of) Kentucky cap, pardner. Like the man says about American Express, I don't leave home without it."

Monday, December 14, 1992

THE LIFE AND TIMES OF C.V. WHITNEY

He was Cornelius Vanderbilt "Sonny" Whitney.

You might see him in the chic, shadowy haze of the Lexington Ball tent, a tall, trim figure in a faultless tuxedo, his bony, patrician face bobbing above the crowd as he danced an anachronistic, expert 1940s-style jitterbug while the Peter Duchin Orchestra blasted out an upbeat disco tune.

Or in the office of his horse farm, where the green pastures seem to roll away to the sky, seated behind his desk, wearing a houndstooth jacket and bolo tie, puffing on — but not inhaling — a menthol cigarette.

He would be fresh from his morning swim and large breakfast (always a large breakfast, a medium lunch and a light dinner — it was one of his rules), and as he gave a visitor a tour of his office and its many silver-framed photographs, he would identify each one in calm, precise, Groton-and-Yale-accented tones:

"And that's Tommy Hitchcock, the world's greatest polo player."

Or again, in places where he often escaped public notice — fishing for bluegill and trout in the mountains of Eastern Kentucky, where he was fascinated by the people and the Appalachian folk art; picnicking with his family at Natural Bridge State Park; or playing cribbage and miniature pool with a staff member in one of the rooms of his farm mansion.

Perhaps the key to Mr. Whitney's life was said as well as anyone could say it by one of his peers, another millionaire horseman, who once remarked:

"He's one of the few men I know who overcame his money. He actually did something with his life."

In an autobiography called *High Peaks* that was published when he was 78, Mr. Whitney wrote: "Generally speaking, movies and TV present rich persons — millionaires — very differently from the life I've led."

And he was a quaint sight that year, sitting patiently in a Lexington department store, signing copies of his book and exchanging chitchat with its buyers, just like any fledgling author.

When he published a later book, titled *Live a Year With a Millionaire!*, *Harper's* magazine lightheartedly illustrated an excerpt from the book with pictures of Little Orphan Annie's Daddy Warbucks and Walt Disney's Scrooge McDuck — because, on the surface, Mr. Whitney was among the super-rich and lived accordingly.

He had his private jet. His 87,000-acre "camp" in the Adirondacks. His Bluegrass horse farm, his Saratoga, N.Y., home, his New York City home, his Florida home, his chalet in Switzerland, his hideaway on Majorca.

And in the 1920s, he had been a famous Long Island playboy, pursued by scandal-sniffing gossip columnists, wooed by chorus girls, courted by the East Coast blueblood party set. He was married to Marie Norton in Paris in 1923, divorced in 1929; married to Gladys Hopkins in Pennsylvania in 1931, divorced in 1941; and that same year married Eleanor Searle, a concert singer.

That, too, ended in divorce, and in 1958 he took his final wife, Marie Louise "Marylou" Hosford, a movie actress. The marriage lasted until his death.

But unlike the idle rich, Mr. Whitney's life unfolded a different way. He was active and accomplished.

He had rowed on the Yale team but also contributed to the college literary magazine. He had inherited $20 million in cash from his father but began his own fortune by parlaying a $3,150 investment in Mexican land.

He didn't merely collect art — he was a talented landscape painter, just as his mother, Gertrude Vanderbilt Whitney, had been a talented sculptor. He didn't merely go to concerts — he was a pianist who had studied under the famous Josef Hoffmann.

He didn't merely play polo well — he also took over his late father's Kentucky horse farm and shrewdly built it into what was, at one time, the finest racing stable in the United States.

He didn't merely found Pan American Airways — during World War I, he had been the youngest instructor in the Army Air Corps; and in World War II, he won flying medals and participated in the assault on Iwo Jima.

Yet he was the same man who could sit down at lunch at the Idle Hour Country Club, order vichyssoise, a grilled cheese sandwich and a Coca-Cola — and then, like any Kentucky country boy, put a handful of peanuts in the Coke.

As one Lexingtonian who knew him observed, "He could have supper in the home of some Eastern Kentucky postmaster during a fishing trip and be just as much at ease as he would have been in the White House — and probably more enthusiastic."

He enjoyed a joke on himself. Once, while dining at a state park in Kentucky, he noticed that all the waitresses were staring at him. Finally, one of them came to the table and told him:

"The other girls and I have a bet. They say you're the one whose house Princess Margaret stayed at when she came to Kentucky. But I bet them you're not. I told them you're the same good old fisherman I've seen here lots of times."

"I'll always remember that you called me a good fisherman," replied Mr. Whitney, "but you do lose the bet."

He was not particularly churchly, but he was religious. There was a chapel at every one of his homes. And on Sunday morning, he would conduct services himself, reading from the Scriptures and leading the hymn singing. During evenings, he enjoyed reading aloud the poetry of Robert W. Service, poems such as *The Shooting* of Dan McGrew.

He loved movies, with Fred Astaire and Ginger Rogers musicals and John Wayne Westerns among his favorites. Sunday night supper at his Lexington home was usually followed by a film, but Mr. Whitney watched for camera angles, editing and other technical points in the movie, for he had, of course, been a Hollywood producer himself.

He had a couple of favorite stories from those days. He enjoyed telling about how, when he had co-produced *Gone With the Wind*, the Hays Office wanted to censor out Clark Gable's immortal line to Vivien Leigh: "Frankly, my dear, I don't give a damn."

Mr. Whitney testified before the censorship committee and won his case.

One of his tactics was showing that the word "damn" was also in the *Bible*.

And then there was the time he was on location with a film crew in the western Badlands, producing a John Wayne epic that John Ford was directing.

Ford was bitten by a scorpion. Members of the film company stood outside the hospital tent, fearing the worst.

Finally, Mr. Whitney sent Wayne into the tent to find out what was happening. Anxious minutes passed. "Then," Mr. Whitney would recall with a smile, "Wayne came out of the tent, held up his hands and said, 'It's OK, fellows — the scorpion died.'"

Mr. Whitney founded Marineland in Florida and had a lifelong fascination with marine biology. "Do you know," he would ask, "that no life form in the ocean ever develops cancer? The future of humanity is there in the sea, if we can find it."

He had sparred with boxing champion Gene Tunney, been a friend of presidents from Franklin Delano Roosevelt to Ronald Reagan, bought horses from the Aga Khan, entertained Princess Margaret as his houseguest — and once, at a casino in Nassau, even gangster Al Capone had begged to be introduced to him (they had a glass of champagne together).

In a sense, he summed up his life during an interview in the 1970s. The interviewer asked him about writer Dorothy Parker, who had, in a memoir she wrote, lovingly recalled the Long Island of the 1920s and the glorious Gatsby-like house parties of C.V. Whitney, nicknamed "Sonny" as a boy because his sisters couldn't pronounce his formidable first name.

Mr. Whitney's blue eyes dimmed for a moment as he searched the memory of a long lifetime ... dozens of countries ... hundreds of parties ... thousands of introductions.

Finally, he cleared his throat and said: "I have no clear recollection of Dottie Parker, but I am sure that I met her. I met everybody."

Those last three words were said without the faintest trace of conceit or snobbery. They were merely a statement of fact.

He had met everybody.

Long-time Herald-Leader staff writer Sue Wahlgren contributed to this column.

Saturday, November 18, 1995

NICK CLOONEY: 'E.R.' STAR'S DAD WAS LEXINGTON HUNK IN '63

Long before there was Hollywood hunk George Clooney, star of *E.R.*, there was his father, Lexington hunk Nick Clooney, star of Coke Time.

And if you were ever on "*School Salute*" on *Coke Time* — well, you're no kid.

"George today is the spitting image of what Nick looked like back then," Andy Wills said.

In 1963, Wills was a 16-year-old Bryan Station High School student who was trying to get a job in television by hanging around *Coke Time*, a WKYT-TV show for teen-agers that Nick Clooney hosted Saturday afternoons.

"It was exactly like Dick Clark's *American Bandstand* show," Wills said.

"Rock 'n' roll music and kids dancing. In fact, one weekend Dick came to Kentucky and did Nick's show and Nick went to Philadelphia and hosted Dick's show."

Back in those days, WKYT was at 1087 New Circle Road NE (where WKQQ radio is today), and Clooney's show was shot live in the parking lot during the summer and inside during cold weather.

Visiting recording artists such as B.J. Thomas (who later sang *Raindrops Keep Fallin' on My Head*) lip-synced their records on the show.

Rock 'n' roll wannabes from Central Kentucky would pantomime songs on the show in hope that somebody in show business would see them and give them a break.

One of these who performed on *Coke Time* — named after its chief sponsor, Coca-Cola — was a teen-ager from Richmond named Jimmy Stokley, who later became lead singer for a band called Exile and had a brief No. 1 hit in 1978 called *Kiss You All Over*.

But most of the guests on the show were just high school students who liked the idea of appearing on a sort of *"Bluegrass Bandstand"* where they could dance, be interviewed and be seen by the folks at home on black-and-white TV.

Clooney, who had married a former Miss Kentucky, was a celebrity with young people in Lexington. He had been a disc jockey at WLAP radio and a popular host at school sock hops. He was, as teen-age girls said in those days, "the living end."

On top of all that, he was the brother of pop singer and Hollywood movie star Rosemary Clooney. The Clooney family was from Maysville, but Nick had at one time attended St. Paul's School in Lexington.

"Nick had the good looks and the great voice that all the Clooneys had," said Frank Faulconer, who was the weather forecaster at WKYT back then.

"He was no singer, but he could do anything in broadcasting and do it well. Kids were mesmerized by him."

Wills, the teen hanger-on of *Coke Time*, did get his start in TV and later became "Happy" of *Happy and Froggy*, a local children's show. "Nick was the greatest friend," he said.

Clooney's *Coke Time* had followed Clark's *American Bandstand* each Saturday on WKYT. Clark's show was an ABC program, but in those days Lexington had only two TV stations. WLEX carried NBC shows and WKYT carried a mix of CBS and ABC programming.

Local teen-agers were sad when Clooney left for larger markets. He hosted a game show in New York called *Money Maze* and was a news anchor in Cincinnati and Los Angeles.

Today, he's the silver-haired host of the cable channel American Movie Classics.

And those old Lexington teens also have gray hair.

And their kids are watching George Clooney.

Friday, January 19, 1996

HUSTLER TOOK CUE FROM BOOK, FILM

Pool hustler Rudolph Wanderone Jr. was fat — but he was no Minnesota Fats, said Walter Tevis.

Wanderone, who died of congestive heart failure yesterday in Nashville, made a career of calling himself Minnesota Fats. He insisted that he inspired the character of Minnesota Fats in a 1961 movie called *The Hustler*.

Tevis grew up in Lexington and graduated from Henry Clay High School and the University of Kentucky. He tried to expose Wanderone's adopted persona, but with little success. He didn't attract as much media attention as Wanderone.

Tevis, who died in 1984, wrote *The Hustler*, the 1959 novel that was the basis for the movie. When the book was reissued in 1976, Tevis wrote a note to the new edition. In part, it said:

"I once saw a fat pool player with a facial tic. I once saw another pool player who was physically graceful. Both were minor hustlers, as far as I could tell. Both seemed loud and vain — with little dignity and grace, unlike my fat pool player. After *The Hustler* was published, one of them claimed to be Minnesota Fats.

"That is ridiculous. I made up Minnesota Fats — name and all — as surely as Disney made up 'Donald Duck.'..."

Why would Wanderone — or anyone — pretend to be a fictional character? The answer is simple: There was money in it.

As Minnesota Fats, Wanderone shot pool on TV with celebrities, wrote books and endorsed pool products such as cues, chalk and tables.

As Rudy Wanderone, who had called himself "New York Fats" prior to

The Hustler movie, he was just another face in the crowd.

Tevis was annoyed by Wanderone's profiteering.

"Why don't you sue him?" I asked Tevis once.

"My lawyer says I have no case," Tevis said. "The novel was copyrighted, but the names of the characters weren't registered as trademarks. If you had wanted to call yourself Huckleberry Finn or David Copperfield, Mark Twain and Charles Dickens couldn't have done anything about it."

Shortly before his death from lung cancer, Tevis finished writing a sequel to *The Hustler*. It was called *The Color of Money*. It was turned into a movie in 1986, starring Paul Newman and Tom Cruise.

Newman had also played the lead role in the 1961 movie. His character was called Fast Eddie Felson. Jackie Gleason had played Minnesota Fats, the old pro that Felson tries to beat at pool. Gleason played the role so well that he was nominated for an Academy Award.

Tevis, who loved to shoot pool and play chess, was a fine writer. One of his science-fiction novels, *The Man Who Fell to Earth*, became a movie starring David Bowie.

Late Lexington pool hall owner Toby Kavanaugh, who taught Tevis to shoot pool and who knew both Tevis and Wanderone, used to say:

"Rudy Wanderone was a big talker and a pretty good gambler. But he wasn't one of the top pool hustlers. And he wasn't Minnesota Fats. Walter made up Minnesota Fats."

In other words, Wanderone hustled a fictional nickname into a career.

So it wasn't really Minnesota Fats who died yesterday in Nashville.

Minnesota Fats lives on in the pages of Tevis' novel and on the strip of celluloid that was Gleason's performance in the film.

Rack 'em.

Tuesday, September 24, 1996

COLONEL HARLAND SANDERS: HIS SPICY SECRET LIFE

OK, four words:

Colonel Sanders' sex life.

If those four words won't keep you reading this column, what does it take?

The real question is: Will they cause you to spend $25 for a new 376-

page book called *The Colonel's Secret?*

The book is subtitled: *Eleven Herbs and a Spicy Daughter.*

That's because the author is Margaret Sanders, eldest daughter of the late Harland Sanders, originator of Kentucky Fried Chicken.

But the colonel's sex life?

The grandfatherly, white-haired old gent in the TV commercials?

Yep, it's one of those books about an American icon where family skeletons come out in public.

For example, Margaret Sanders, now 86, writes about her father's mistress, a divorced woman with two children, who Sanders (what a salesman!) actually talked his wife into hiring to "help her with the housework." The book relates:

"It was evident from the beginning that her presence would create turmoil ... The peace of our whole family was altered by their affair.

"Mother refused to accept that she alone could not satisfy Father's physical needs, which from the very beginning of their marriage had seemed excessive to her..."

Later, she writes, Sanders divorced his wife and married his mistress — and then took both women to Washington, D.C., with him to attend a presidential inauguration.

(Hey, would this guy have fit into the Clinton administration or what?)

And that was just the beginning. Here, as written by his daughter, is a snapshot of the colonel toward the end of his life:

"Noah Dietrich, the famous associate of the even more famous Howard Hughes, lived across the street from me (in Palm Springs).

"Noah's wife, Mary, the grandmother of Bridget Fonda, brought Noah over to my house ... Father was approaching 90 and Noah was 92. They sat with their canes shoved down beside them ... swapping tales with loud guffaws.

"Suddenly, during a lull in our conversation, we heard Father say, 'Noah, I had sex until my 83rd birthday. How long did you have sex?'

"We ladies gasped, waiting for the answer. To Noah's great fortune and Mary's relief, the doorbell rang ..."

Well, well. Maybe there IS some secret ingredient in that fried chicken, after all.

But some readers of the book might disagree with Margaret Sanders' description of herself as the "spicy" daughter.

Perhaps "flaky" would be a better adjective. This is, after all, a woman who searched for the lost continent of Atlantis, tried to add to Einstein's theory of relativity, takes credit for "the revolutionary concept" of take-out fried chicken stores and was married five times.

She is a talented artist. It's her sculpture of her father that overlooks his grave in a Louisville cemetery.

And she's a pretty good storyteller. The book is full of family photos, personal revelations and memorable anecdotes, such as the time Colonel Sanders spotted a hard-working table buser in a fried chicken restaurant in Indianapolis and predicted that the kid would be a big success one day.

He was right. The table buser turned out to be Dave Thomas, who later founded Wendy's and, like Sanders, starred in his own ads.

There are enough spicy secrets for readers to talk about.

But please. No "finger-lickin'-good" jokes.

Thursday, September 11, 1997

SHAKING OUT AN ANSWER TO SANDERS' SPICY RIDDLE

The most famous secret recipe in the history of Kentucky is the "11 secret herbs and spices" in Col. Harland Sanders' fried chicken.

But is it really a secret — or just a mystery?

I grew up eating the fried chicken that was served at Sanders' original "court and cafe" (motel and restaurant) that stood next to U.S. 25 on the north side of Corbin.

What was in that stuff? The colonel himself once said that the ingredients could be found on anybody's kitchen shelf.

Ray Kroc, founder of the McDonald's restaurants, was quoted in 1976 as saying that the colonel's so-called secret was not really a secret to modern science.

"Any laboratory can tell you what's in it," said Kroc. "There's no platinum in there. There's no gold in there."

In 1983, a book called *Big Secrets* by William Poundstone claimed to have commissioned just such a lab test.

The book reported that "nothing was found that couldn't be identified" and that only three seasoning ingredients were found in the lab analysis:

Salt, pepper and a big helping of monosodium glutamate .

Maybe it was a dead point, anyway.

Sanders had sold his Kentucky Fried Chicken business in 1964. His daughter, Margaret Sanders, later wrote a book in which she said her father's original recipe had been "reformulated" by the new owners' food engineer.

So what were the original "11 secret herbs and spices" used by Sanders in his original restaurant?

Well, as Damon Runyon said, "The race is not always to the swift or the battle to the strong — but that's the way to bet."

Here's my bet: I think the colonel's secret was salt, pepper and MSG — plus poultry seasoning.

Yes, plain old poultry seasoning. You can find some variety of it in any spice section at any supermarket.

It's a ground-up mixture of 10 or 11 herbs and spices such as sage, thyme, nutmeg, cayenne, cilantro, savory, etc.

I would bet on it for three reasons:

• It's consistent with ingredients that were available in Corbin at the time the recipe was developed.

• It's consistent with what Sanders said about the ingredients being on any cook's shelf.

• And it's consistent with a recipe for fried chicken that was written in a private letter a long time ago by a Corbin woman named Eula Gibson.

She worked for Sanders 50 years ago and may have co-created the recipe that later became so famous, even though she never got public credit for it.

Who knows how many different recipes and combinations of seasonings were experimented with in those old days?

When the government awarded Sanders a patent for his way of fixing chicken, the patent was for the cooking process, not for the recipe.

Some of it remains a mystery that will never be solved. And these days, who really cares what the ingredients are?

Most people buy their fried chicken by the box and bucket. Hardly anybody still cooks it at home, and kids grow up thinking that a chicken is something that comes from a drive-through window.

You can even get fried chicken at some Wal-Mart stores.

That is ironic, given that when Sanders began franchising his product, skeptics asked:

"Who'll go to a restaurant to buy what they can cook at home?"

As it turned out, just about everybody.

Thursday, June 26, 1986

FRIED-CHICKEN KING IS CARRYING ON A FAMILY TRADITION

These fried-chicken kings are colorful birds. There sat Lee Cummings, 63, his diamond-studded Rolex wristwatch sparkling in the sunshine, his broad, rooster-decorated suspenders curving down over his rotund form.

He was signing complimentary cards — "Have One On Me At Lee's Famous Recipe" — that entitle the bearer .o "dinner for one."

There was a slight incongruity to this. On the line of the card that read "Location," Cummings was writing "Knoxville" with his ballpoint pen.

The incongruity was that Cummings was in Lexington, 200 miles from Knoxville.

He spends so much time on the road promoting the product that he can't always remember which city he's visiting.

"I'm gonna be just like the Colonel," he said. "I don't want to retire."

Maybe it's in the genes. Colonel Harland Sanders, founder of Kentucky Fried Chicken, was Cummings' uncle.

"Harland was my mother's brother," he said. "I think they ran him out of Indiana for bootlegging. I was working for him in Corbin in 1948. The Colonel worked you hard. He was always kind of upset that there wasn't more than 24 hours in a day and seven days in a week.

"And I was working for him when we started franchising the chicken. After he sold the business, I started my own. Really, the chicken business was the only thing I knew."

In 1966, Cummings and his brother-in-law, Harold Omer, opened Harold's Take Home, featuring Cummings' Famous Recipe, in a converted gas station in Lima, Ohio. A year later, he had 18 restaurants going. Twenty years later, the Famous Recipe chain has 262 restaurants in 24 states, Malaysia and Trinidad.

Cummings sold Famous Recipe to Nashville-based Shoney's Inc. for $2.2 million in 1981. Now he travels around as "official spokesperson" on the Famous Recipe payroll. This sounds like a clone of his uncle; Sanders built up Kentucky Fried Chicken, then sold it and became KFC's traveling image man.

The question is, how much of a clone is Cummings' Famous Recipe recipe from Sanders' old Kentucky Fried Chicken recipe? Cummings admits that he knew Sanders' so-called "11 secret herbs and spices" formula.

"Of course I knew it," he said. "I used to mix it — I had to prepare it and blend it many a time. But our recipe is quite a bit different. We have about five ingredients. And we use a different pressure-cooker timing."

Cummings was asked about a book of a couple of years ago called *Big Secrets*.

The author said that he had obtained a sample of the Kentucky Fried Chicken formula and that an exhaustive laboratory analysis revealed only three ingredients: salt, pepper and a large amount of monosodium glutamate.

"That guy needs to analyze it again," Cummings said. "Salt and pepper and MSG — those are your basics. But there's more to it than that. Sure, you can put a formula through a lab and find out what's in it — but what a lab can't do is balance it out. The secret is how much of each ingredient you use, how one spice balances the flavor of another."

The Famous Recipe promotional ads tout Cummings as "the world's foremost authority on country cooking."

Somehow the words "country cooking" do not bring to mind dehydrated potatoes, which Cummings admitted that Famous Recipe uses in its gravy-mashed potato mixture.

"Well, they're good if you fix 'em right," Cummings said. "The water's got to be boiling and you have to whip some air into 'em."

Why not use fresh potatoes? he was asked.

"Laborwise, you can't do that anymore," he replied.

Cummings says he eats "98.2 percent" of his meals at fast-food restaurants, usually at Famous Recipe or Shoney's. But he doesn't eat as much as he once did.

"I've been on a diet," he said. "I lost 36 pounds. I had no choice. I had to lose weight — I'm diabetic. But I don't have a cholesterol problem, I'll tell you that. Now come on over here and try some of these Famous Recipe vegetables. And our Extra-Crispy. Have you tried our Extra-Crispy?"

Friday, June 5, 1992

LEAVE STATE TO BECOME A FAMOUS KENTUCKIAN

In a way, I hate to see these big, historical state celebrations like bicentennials.

It means that somebody will bring up the subject of famous Kentuckians.

And if you look at famous Kentuckians, you are soon struck by the fact that nearly all of them (1) weren't Kentuckians to begin with, or (2) left Kentucky and became famous elsewhere.

That makes the rest of us non-famous Kentuckians look like dopes for staying here.

No matter. Here they are — some famous Kentuckians (?) to brag about:

1. Stephen Foster, composer of *My Old Kentucky Home*, was from Pittsburgh, and never lived in Kentucky. The only house still standing in which Foster ever lived is in Hoboken, N.J.

2. Col. Harland Sanders, originator of Kentucky Fried Chicken, was born, grew up and learned to cook in Indiana.

3. Abraham Lincoln left Kentucky as a child, grew up in Illinois, became famous in Washington, D.C., and never won an election in Kentucky.

4. Daniel Boone was born in Pennsylvania, grew up in North Carolina and moved to Kentucky, where he was tried for treason, lost all his land and lost a son and brother who were killed by Indians. He moved to Missouri, where he died after a huge meal of sweet potatoes.

5. Carry Nation, hatchet-wielding prohibitionist, left Kentucky for Missouri at age 9, and became famous many years later for chopping up saloons.

6. Christopher "Kit" Carson, famous frontier scout, moved away from Kentucky with his parents when he was a baby, and did his famous scouting in the West.

7. Henry Clay was born in Virginia, and became famous in Washington, D.C., where he died.

8. Cassius Clay became a famous professional boxer, then changed his name to Muhammad Ali and left Louisville for Los Angeles and later Michigan.

9. Robert Penn Warren, distinguished writer who won three Pulitzer Prizes, left Kentucky as a teen-ager to go to college in Tennessee and only came back to visit.

10. Man o' War, the famous racehorse whose statue is at the Kentucky Horse Park, was bred by a New York millionaire, sold as a yearling at Saratoga, and never raced in Kentucky.

HORSE BIZ

Keeneland. Churchill Downs. Majestic farms sweeping across the rolling hills of the Bluegrass. These conjure up that magical — and sometimes mystifying — world of thoroughbred racing. To people around the world, the horse is the symbol of Kentucky's distinctiveness. Yet this world keeps changing at an unrelenting pace. Today, no farm stands tall and regal as Calumet did at its height. To many Lexingtonians, Hamburg Place, the farm, is now confused, at best, with Hamburg Pavilion, the shopping center. Betting, with its many options and combinations, is more bewildering than ever, and the possible arrival of slot machines would make today's racetracks unrecognizable to their founders. The old, traditional track, now long gone, seems destined to become what Don Edwards calls "Keno-Land, a place where gambling had wiped out racing." One thing that has not changed: A bet is never a sure thing.

Thursday, April 15, 1999

AH, THOSE DERBY SECRETS

To the outside world, we sit under a pink and white dogwood tree, sip mint juleps in Churchill Downs souvenir glasses and call one another "colonel."

And on the first Saturday in May, we link arms and tearfully sing *My Old Kentucky Home* amid the flash and color of big hats and Hollywood celebrities.

Then the starting gate opens, "They're off!" and we risk a stroke from the excitement of watching the lead change ... and change ... and change.

Then "DOWN the stretch they come!" with thundering hooves, horse-flesh straining toward the finish line of "the greatest two minutes in sports," "the run for the roses" or any other cliche´ of your choice.

Whew! After the post-race interviews, the eight hours of TV programming are finally over and our secrets are safe for another 364 days.

The secrets are stuff that all Kentuckians know but never talk about on TV because the rest of the world is watching.

If they did, the TV commentary might sound like this:

"The crowd is preparing to sing *My Old Kentucky Home* now, Chuck. It's been called the most emotional moment in American sports. Just look at those faces."

"Yes, Rick. They're trying to concentrate. Most of them don't know all the words of their state song even when they aren't sloshed on bad mint juleps."

"Really, Chuck?"

"Yes, Rick. Most Kentuckians have never actually been to the Derby. Probably half of them couldn't tell you which horse won last year.

"And if you really want to see some blank faces, ask them which horse won five years ago."

"How do you know all this, Chuck?"

"The same way I know all those celebrities are here because they didn't have to pay to get in. It's worldwide publicity for doing nothing, Rick."

"Just who is the most important person here today, Chuck?"

"To the average Derby-goer who wants to be where the movie stars and millionaires are, it's the ticket scalper, Rick.

"There are some clubhouse table holders who haven't been to the race in years because they scalp every Derby. After all, you can watch the whole thing free on TV."

"But that's not like being there to see a race in person, Chuck."

"No, it isn't. Rick. That's why some of the ticket holders who scalp the Derby go to the Oaks, the featured race on Friday. But the Oaks is now so popular as part of the weekend package that it's being scalped more often."

"Well, how about that? Now let's go live to our turf expert, Amelia, who earlier today spent two hours showing us a tiny percentage of the commercial tie-ins at the track. Maybe one day it'll be called 'The Papa John's Pizza Kentucky Derby.'

"Now she's going to give us her last-second prediction. Who'll be the winner? What do you say, Amelia?"

"Menifee! Back to you, Rick and Chuck."

"Thanks, Amelia. What high excitement. Just look at this spectacle, Chuck. What a race! What a tradition! And what more could Churchill Downs possibly want?"

"Slot machines," says Chuck.

(Note to all Kentuckians: If you can't remember last year's Derby winner or the winner five years ago, the answers are Real Quiet and Go for Gin.)

Thursday, October 23, 1986

EQUINE AURAS PUT PSYCHIC TO THE TEST AT KEENELAND

I went through the gates of Keeneland Race Course yesterday like a sheep with steel wool. Instead of the parimutuel windows fleecing me as usual, I figured that I was going to do the fleecing.

In fact, if it worked out as I planned, I was going to bust the track so badly that Keeneland board Chairman James E. "Ted" Bassett III would have to hock his Rolex.

Naturally, I had a secret weapon. After having tried — and failed with — everything else at Keeneland, I was banking on the cosmos, the stars, kismet, fate, vibes.

In other words, I was taking a psychic with me to pick the horses.

"An animal has a different kind of aura than people do," Wanda Ellington said as she intently studied the horses for the first race. "You look for the energy. A horse aura is like wavy lines, like heat rising." Wanda is the shopping center psychic at the Festival Market. She's a pro.

The only thing I was worried about was whether her psychic powers had been corrupted by dubious outside influences.

Lately, I had heard, she had been picking college football games with (*Herald-Leader* columnist) D.G. FitzMaurice at Scores restaurant. FitzMaurice had even put up a chart labeled "Wanda the Psychic vs. Fitz the Psycho." I didn't like the sound of that, but I figured the cosmos could overcome it.

I mean, if it's in the stars, it must be on the track, too, right? In the first race, Wanda initially liked Main Angle's looks. "But that might just be because of the color of the horse," she said. She also thought Crimson Bar had a good-looking aura. I squinted, trying to see auras myself. All I could see were bobbing, chestnut-colored rumps and heads.

I bet on Crimson Bar. Main Angle won and paid $14.20. I was not discouraged.

She had picked Main Angle. I should have stuck with that horse. There were seven more races to go. I was gonna clean up. I could feel it in my bones.

In the second race, Wanda liked Juliet's Love and Setting. I bet on Setting.

Fire Break won it. I was not discouraged. Psychics are the first to tell you that they're not 100 percent accurate; nobody is. Fire Break paid only a lousy $3.20, anyway.

The third race looked like a quick way to get well. Deal Me Spades had a lovely aura. Just to be cautious, I bet on him to show. Valid Prospect won and paid $79. Deal Me Spades, aura and all, finished out of the money.

I lost the fourth race, too. It would have been a good one to win. Son Plaisir won it and paid $47.20.

In the fifth race, Wanda perked up. "Number 1 and Number 5 both look very good," she said. "But I think I like Number 5 a little better. Red is a physically energizing color." No. 5 was a filly named Frisky Kitten. The jockey was wearing red silks.

No. 1 was a filly named Sheena Native. It was four minutes to post time. I almost knocked three people down getting to the parimutuel window and laid $20 on the nose of Frisky Kitten and $2 on Sheena Native.

Well, she was frisky. But not frisky enough. She ran second. Sheena Native won and paid a measly $4.60. But Wanda had picked both horses. "She's warming up," I thought. "I can still come out of this — all I need is that one big longshot."

The sixth race looked like the one. Wanda studied the equine auras. It came down to two horses named Silent Force and The Flats. Silent Force was going off at about 50 to 1. My heart leaped. I hastened to the window, money in hand.

Rare Brick won it. The Flats ran second. For all I know, Silent Force, that bum, is still running.

There were two races left. In the seventh, Wanda spotted a good aura hovering above Christmas Dancer. It was a 12-to-1 shot. "It's now or never," I thought.

I went to the window; a $20 bill changed hands.

They were off. Christmas Dancer took the lead. I was screaming. Then something happened.

Coax Me Molly won. Christmas Dancer ran third. Wanda had bet on Christmas Dancer, too. "I guess it goes to show," she said, "that even if you're psychic, you can't second-guess horses." It was time for the last race. It was a 12-horse field and loaded with auras.

I bet on three of them. Tanya's Roberto was the one I needed to win. If the horse did win, I could still break even. Wanda bet on Bald Witch.

For one final time, the cosmos double-crossed us, the stars let us down and kismet kissed us off.

Delta Daiquiry won the race.

On the way out of the track I glanced in the rear-view mirror and almost wrecked the car. Suddenly I saw it! I saw my aura! It looked like a flat tire. In fact, it looked just like my wallet.

Sunday, March 22, 1992

■ Calumet Farm was sold at auction March 26, 1992.

A TIMELESS LEGACY

In the old days, if Lexington had been the British Isles, Calumet Farm would have been its Buckingham Palace.

It had a king and queen — Warren Wright Sr. and Lucille Wright.

Later, the king died, and the queen took a new husband. Then it was Gene Markey and Lucille Markey.

It had its crown jewels — Triple Crown jewels, more than 500 gold and silver racing trophies that filled their own room — for its racing stable was second to none.

Like Buckingham Palace, it could be visited by commoners. Tourists in those days were free to walk behind its white fences and snap photos of its blueblooded horses.

It had been on Versailles Road since 1924, before Keeneland Race Course, before Blue Grass Airport. But its golden age began in 1941 when its horse, Whirlaway, won the Triple Crown. It ended in 1982 with the death of Lucille Markey.

Calumet was a very American institution. It was built on a baking-powder fortune and named for an Indian peace pipe.

Everyone in Lexington was proud of it. In its field, the breeding of thoroughbred yearlings for the racetrack, it was as good as anything in the world.

World-class endeavors were rare in Kentucky. There was the UK basketball team that won the gold medal at the 1948 Olympic Games, and there were famous horses and farms.

Calumet was the top of the heap, the epitome of class. It seemed to live in an eternal spring of mint juleps on silver trays, with gentlemen in houndstooth jackets and ladies in white hats and gloves the shade of dogwood blossoms.

Hollywood shot movies there. Stars such as John Wayne visited. Some of the movies were based on novels by Gene Markey, who had been a Hollywood screenwriter married to — and divorced from — Joan Bennett, Hedy Lamarr and Myrna Loy.

He was a bon vivant whose motto was, "We live only once, and even that might be too often." He liked being called Admiral, liked the Rolls-Royce his wife gave him, liked flying in other people's private planes and liked partying in Europe with dukes and earls.

Legally, the Markeys were Florida residents. For a time, they had a home in Bel-Air in Los Angeles. They would spend winter in Miami Beach, the spring racing season in Kentucky, summer at the Ritz in Paris, August at Saratoga and their entire marriage on the society pages.

They weren't above staging an image to project. An old Calumet Christmas card shows them solemnly playing chess in the farm's gleaming trophy room. On close inspection, one notices that the chessboard is set up backward.

In old age, she became nearly blind and he became her eyes. She still carped about how the house in Kentucky needed cleaning. "I can feel the dust," she insisted.

When they died, she left millions to children's charities and cancer research.

He left his old pal Douglas Fairbanks Jr. a set of Oriental pearl studs, cuff links and waistcoat buttons.

He was quite different from her first husband, Warren Wright Sr. Wright was the consummate businessman. When he ran Calumet, it raised cattle, had a dairy, sold butter and eggs. He was not the kind of man who would mix rum punch, wear a beret and dance to *La Cucaracha*. When he spoke about Calumet, it was in the first person singular. He lived to see most of the Calumet glory horses that won the Derby in the 1940s: Whirlaway, Pensive, Citation and Ponder. He died in 1950, so he missed Hill Gail, Iron Liege, Tim Tam and Forward Pass. And he never got to know Alydar.

He enjoyed glory, but he kept score with money, so he would have loved Alydar's designer genes. And he would have loved the record. By 1958, the Calumet racing stable had led all winning owners for the 11th time since 1941.

In 1958, its racing stable earned nearly $1 million in a year when a quarter would buy a loaf of bread.

Wright left his widow as the farm's tenant for her lifetime, which is as long as anyone has anything. She could have sold it, but was never seriously interested in being merely one more rich lady when she could be queen of Calumet Farm. As she said in 1959: "No one has enough money to buy it, anyway." As planes replaced trains, Calumet's undulating pastures, storybook white fences and stately red and white barns became a Lexington hallmark — the first horse farm that visitors saw as they flew into town. Its picture was in the city directory.

The heart of something wonderful is the feeling that it can't happen again.

There was always that feeling about Calumet in the years when it completely dominated racing in a way that no other farm in history had managed to do.

You knew it couldn't last. You knew that either the farm would change or racing would change, and you took a ticket on the farm changing.

In Oscar Wilde's book, *The Picture of Dorian Gray*, the hero stays the same in appearance while his portrait ages and withers.

In the old days, the people of Central Kentucky looked into Calumet like a mirror. They tried to find themselves in its reflected glory, and they tried to define their community there, too.

The people grew older, but the fences stayed white and the grass green. It was a portrait that seemed eternal. When Calumet finally aged, then limped, then fell to Earth, it was almost unimaginable.

Tuesday, January 20, 1998

THERE IS NO REQUIEM FOR THIS OLD HORSE FARM

"Horses Have Right of Way."
— Old road sign on Hamburg Place farm.

When a piece of a jigsaw puzzle is changed, the whole puzzle changes.

On a map of Lexington, a huge chunk of the puzzle is the 1,900 acres of mostly open space bounded by New Circle, Winchester and Liberty roads and Man o' War Boulevard.

In land size, it's as large as several Lexington neighborhoods put together — big enough to be its own Urban County Council district, except that the population has been mostly equine for the past century.

This is Hamburg Place, the horse farm founded by John E. Madden in 1898.

That centennial mark is not going unnoticed this year. The farm's famous Madden Derby Eve party will have a 100th birthday as its party theme.

Eleven years ago, the farm bell atop the water tower was ringing in celebration of Alysheba, the 1987 Derby and Preakness winner.

He was to be the last great horse at a farm that had produced six Derby winners and the first Triple Crown winner.

This year, the bell of history tolls for Hamburg Place. Most of the land is on its way to becoming a mixed-use real estate development.

Unlike some Fayette County horse farms that have vanished without a trace, this one is a planned community with a legacy.

As part of that plan, last week the Madden family announced it would give Lexington 50 acres for a new park and new school adjacent to Liberty Road.

It was a bow to tradition. Hamburg Place has long been a shared place and a part of the larger community.

Sixty years ago, Girl Scouts used the farm as a campground. The Iroquois Polo Club played matches there, and there was a kids' polo team, too, with little silver cups for the winners.

A visiting football team in town to play the University of Kentucky worked out on the polo field. Teenagers learning to drive cars started out on the polo field because they couldn't hit anything there.

There were prestigious events and ordinary ones, too. The Prince of Wales Steeplechase was run there and the local pony club rode there.

There was a horse cemetery that tourists visited. The farm had its own racetrack that was used as a setting in a Hollywood movie.

There were the anomalies of war. During the World War II era, Hamburg Place grew 200 acres of hemp by government mandate. German prisoners of war being held at nearby Avon worked on the farm housing the tobacco crop.

Over the years, there were charity fund-raisers, political fund-raisers, art league exhibitions, Urban League dinners and, of course, parties.

The Derby Eve became the best known, but there were many others.

Parties with dancing and fireworks, parties with Ferris wheels and merry-go-rounds.

Parties with movie stars, millionaires and maharajahs. Parties with costumed mermaids in the Olympic-size swimming pool.

Parties to benefit the UK wrestling team and to help celebrate the Kentucky State University centennial.

The biggest party of all was the NCAA Final Four party of 1985, with an estimated crowd of 4,000 to 5,000.

This is no requiem for an old horse farm, but after four generations and 100 years, the changing of this piece of the Lexington jigsaw really does change the look of the whole puzzle.

Sunday, January 17, 1999

THIS IS ONE GAMBLE THAT KEENELAND CANNOT WIN

Watching Keeneland Race Course jump into bed with a casino company is like watching your 63-year-old aunt go to work for an escort service.

That's what it looks like Keeneland is doing — escorting casinos into Kentucky's future because they haven't been able to get in by themselves.

On Friday, the race course announced that it is an equal partner with a subsidiary of GTECH Corp. and Harrah's in a deal to buy Turfway Park in Florence for $37 million.

Keeneland said the deal was for "the good of racing."

Is there an echo in this state? In Louisville, Churchill Downs says it wants slot machines "to save racing" from riverboat casinos.

What a pair of saviors Keeneland has hooked up with. GTECH runs lotteries, including the one in Kentucky, and Harrah's runs 20 gambling casinos.

Depending on these guys to save racing sounds like depending on Colonel Sanders to save chickens.

"Racing as it was meant to be" has been Keeneland's self-satisfied motto.

What will it be after this? "Gambling as it's going to be."

Until now, Keeneland has fought in Frankfort to keep casino gambling off the public ballot. The track was against casino gambling "at this time."

A new time has suddenly been ushered in. Bill Greely, Keeneland's president, said Friday that he thinks "the people of Kentucky should decide."

They decided a long time ago. That's why casino gambling has been illegal in Kentucky all these years.

Racing was excepted and had a monopoly on legal gambling until the lottery came in.

Should we amend our state constitution so people can play slot machines at racetracks?

This sounds like Keeneland and its new pals, GTECH and Harrah's, are looking toward a near-monopoly on legal gambling.

If you buy a lottery ticket, they vacuum up the money. If you bet at Keeneland or Turfway, they vacuum up the money. And if you play slot machines in the future, they'll vacuum up that, too.

What they don't get, Churchill Downs will.

The tracks think they can let the casino-gambling genie out of the bottle as long they control it.

It won't stop with slot machines. Casino money ultimately will buy racing because it's bigger money than racing ever thought of.

Letting it into Kentucky is not an inoculation that will "save racing" — it's a cancer that will destroy racing by eventually turning tracks into casinos.

Twenty years ago, if you had predicted that convenience stores and supermarkets would turn into gambling sites with the state's blessing, some people would have thought you were crazy.

But that's just what happened 10 years later with the Kentucky Lottery.

Now Keeneland and the lottery vendor have combined with a casino gambling company to buy a Northern Kentucky track that Keeneland wouldn't have sniffed down its nose at a few years ago.

Is it so hard to guess that Keeneland — rather like a Bluegrass debutante who becomes a stripper to save the old family fortune — is speculating on the casino business?

On Aug. 8, 1990, in this space, we wrote a speculative column about what Keeneland would look like in the year 2010.

We predicted it would be called Keno-Land, a place where gambling had wiped out racing.

Almost halfway there, it's starting to look like a pretty good bet.

Tuesday, April 19, 1994

LIFE IS LIKE A HORSE RACE

Last week at the Keeneland clubhouse, a woman was standing in line at a parimutuel window when her slip fell down around her ankles.

"I've heard of people losing their shirts here," said the dining room maitre d', "but I'd never seen anybody lose a slip." As the railbirds would say, she "broke sharply" and "showed in the stretch." And on Sunday at Keeneland, there was a horse in the fifth race named: Blondeintheshower.

Yeah, you read it right. And guess who was listed in the Keeneland program as the owner — Gov. Brereton C. Jones.

Maybe he doesn't want to reveal who his partners are in those horse deals, but would it be even more interesting if he would reveal who's picking those names? Just kidding. Blondeintheshower has an equine ancestor named Bates Motel.

That's the fictional motel where Janet Leigh was the blonde in the shower in the old movie, Psycho.

Forget Oprah, Dear Abby and your psychiatrist. You can hear all of life summed up in the horse notes at the track.

In fact, that's why I go there.

I don't go for the food, the drinks, the gossip and the gambling (ha, ha, ha).

I go for the philosophy.

Life is like a horse race.

When you were young, you "loomed boldly" and "closed willingly" and "finished well."

Or maybe you didn't. Maybe you were a "fractious loader" who "broke slowly" and was "no threat." Perhaps you even "trailed throughout." Or maybe you "failed to respond."

Maiden races are the toughest to pick. No past performance records. You can't know for sure how young horses might turn out — but there are good signs and bad signs. Isn't it that way with people, too?

In middle age, did you "set the pace, then weaken" and "faded in the stretch"? Or were you "much the best" but "failed to sustain bid"?

And in old age, when the shadows had grown long in the paddock and it was post time for the last race, perhaps you were "far back with no rally" and "never in contention." Or maybe you were just "ridden out."

You could pick an epitaph from all this stuff: "Clearly second best." "No speed." "Showed little." "Lacked late response." "Used up." "Outrun."

Hey, it wouldn't have to be a total downer. There are also: "Never far back." "Passed tiring rivals." "Best stride late." "Outfinished gamely." "Just missed."

What a way to go. If I should die at the track, please tell everybody I "gave way late." Don't mention the part about "mild rally" and "never fired."

In the old days, there was a Lexington bookie who used to say that he was tired of being a bookie. He said he really wanted to retire, but his customers wouldn't let him.

"Nobody's willing to quit a winner," he said. "No matter how much they come out ahead, they come back the next day and bet it all again."

I'm afraid he was right. That's the way most of us are, whether we win going away or get scratched.

DAYS GONE BY

Life's fondest memories often go back to childhood. Years later, an adult may look back with longing toward lazy summer days of June bug flying or melon thumping, or Halloween mischief when it was safe and innocent, or learning to play chess. Perhaps childhood's deepest lesson can only be learned as an adult, upon a return to the scene of one's youth. In encounters with the ghosts of long ago, there is a bittersweet reminder that the past, no matter how cherished, is indeed past. There may also be a reminder that home is still where the heart is, even if that heart is far away.

Monday, August 17, 1987

THE LOST ARTS OF SUMMER

Kids used to be happier this time of year because summer vacation lasted until Labor Day.

Back then, nobody in his right mind thought that any public school should open before any public swimming pool closed.

That was one of the lost arts of summer — making vacations last longer.

There are other lost arts, too.

Such as melon thumping. That is, thumping a watermelon to see if it's ripe on the inside.

At Farmers' Market in Lexington, you can see people hit, slap, pinch, prod and karate-kick watermelons.

A mere thump of the fingernail does it. If you get a ping, it's green. If you get a thud, it's ripe.

And will somebody please stand up and be counted as a practitioner of the lost art of June bug flying? It was the cheapest, most simple-minded entertainment around. You tied a long thread to a June bug's leg and held on while the beetle flew in circles, buzzing like an airplane.

Parents today are reluctant to tell their kids that they once did such things, for two reasons:

First, the kids would think the parents suffered a deficit of intelligence.

Second, the kids would say: "We are like totally not into insect bondage and please don't bother us now because we are like running an important program on our PC."

There are other lost arts of summer, such as making lemonade without NutraSweet, pushing a lawn mower that has no engine, riding a bicycle with only one gear and swinging in a hammock without falling out.

Life was more mysterious back then. You had to try to guess which brands of clothes people were wearing because you couldn't see the labels.

There were challenges, too. One challenge was to try to find anything made in Japan that wasn't cheap.

These days, one of the greatest lost arts is getting exercise without jogging. Another is listening to a radio that is not attached to your head.

And another is sitting on a front porch in the evening and doing no more than saying hello to people as they walk past on the sidewalk.

That last one is close to the greatest of all lost arts of summer — namely, the art of doing absolutely nothing and not feeling guilty about it.

Today when people tell you they're doing absolutely nothing, you just can't trust them.

It always turns out that they're watching TV or talking on a cordless telephone.

Thursday, October 26, 1995

HALLOWEEN MCGUFFINS

I like to see those fat orange pumpkins and crayon-colored autumn leaves.

Just before the sun sinks in a rosy hue, the horizon turns dark. Across its edge, maybe you can see a witch flying on a broom with fire shooting out of the broom tail.

It was just this time of year that Kentucky teen-agers would begin planning the McGuffin.

The McGuffin was a sort of con game. It was played among friends and it had a simple object — to scare the holy kraut out of its victims.

Once there were lots of old abandoned houses in Central Kentucky, many more than now. These places became theaters of the McGuffin.

There were a couple such places in the Bluegrass that later became famous.

One was Shakertown in Mercer County. Before it was restored and became a tourist mecca, it looked exactly like a ghost town. In those days, the main highway ran right through the middle of it. Coming onto the old, empty village on a dark night, even Stephen King would have thought twice before getting out of the car.

The other place was the abandoned Whitehall mansion in Madison County. It stood alone in near-ruin. Not even a road ran to it anymore. You had to climb a fence and walk across a pasture to reach it.

Its late owner, Cassius M. Clay, had killed men with pistols and bowie knives. There was a folk story that he had gone insane and turned snakes loose in the house.

When you hear about a place like that, you're halfway scared before you even get there.

The McGuffin worked this way: At dusk, three of you would take a new member of the club (the victim) to a scary old house. The new member would prove his or her courage by entering the house, climbing to a second-story window and waving a white handkerchief out the window so that the others could see it.

What actually happened was this: Before you went to the house, two of you took the victim to pick up the third member of the escort party. But the third member couldn't go; he said he was stuck having to do homework.

So the two of you took the victim and left. You dawdled around and went the long way to the old house. Meanwhile, the one who'd said he couldn't go because of homework was taking a short cut to the old house. He was going to get there first, and be upstairs in a closet by that window waiting for the victim.

When the victim waved the white handkerchief out the window and turned to leave, the third member was standing silently in front of him wearing a horrible face mask.

If you could hear the victim's blood-curdling scream all the way down to the ground, the McGuffin was declared a success.

There was also a Double McGuffin, where the victim and the friend planted in the house conspired to scare the other two of you — usually by the victim pretending to be dead from fright after finding the horrible-looking fake-blood-splattered "dead body" of the one planted inside the house.

There was even a Triple McGuffin, but it was so complicated that I can't remember how it went. I think it involved using a pistol with blank cartridges.

Halloween pranks seemed like a lot more fun back then.

The old McGuffin days were not perfect. But you didn't have to worry about real bullets in drive-by shootings and razor blades in the trick-or-treat candy.

Tuesday, March 28, 1995

'IN CHESS YOU HAVE TO BE YOUR PIECES'

When Elliott Fleming was 2 years old, he memorized all 56 lines of the poem that begins: "Twas the night before Christmas... ."

When he was 3, his parents, Kermin and Debra Fleming of Lexington, noticed that he could add numbers up into the thousands in his head.

He wasn't old enough to explain how he did it. He could just do it and that was that.

"Elliott has never liked explaining the obvious," his mother says.

When he was 4, he learned to play chess. A lot of things happened after that.

Elliott was 9 when I first noticed him at a school club. By then he was already a chess monster, beating most of the other kids and the teachers, too.

He played chess like a video game. Five seconds a move. He'd sacrifice his queen — then WHAM! — roar his knights, bishops and rooks down the board in a mad rush to checkmate the enemy king.

"In chess," he told me confidently, "you have to be your pieces."

"What do you mean by that?" I asked him.

"You have to see the squares the same way your pieces see them," he said in a bored voice.

"C'mon, let's play. One minute!"

When two players set their clocks at one minute, each has 60 seconds to make all his moves in the game or he loses on time. In other words, you play an entire game of chess in the same amount of time it takes the horses to run around the track in the Kentucky Derby.

The kid was cocky, but I felt like a piano teacher discovering a little would-be Mozart. Just fooling around, he was easily one of the most gifted young players I had run across.

What might he be if he really worked at the game?

That was two years ago. I got my answer Sunday in Louisville at the Kentucky scholastic chess championships, a two-day tournament.

Steve Dillard, the tournament director, held up a big, glittering trophy and said: "And now, undisputed, unbeaten, untied — the 1995 elementary school chess champion of Kentucky: Elliott Fleming."

Elliott, who is a fifth grader at Julia R. Ewan Elementary School, got his trophy and had his photo taken. Then he looked at his parents and said, "I'm hungry."

Kimberly Fleming, his unimpressed younger sister, pointed to her brother and said in a deadpan voice: "The bottomless pit."

Elliott's father is rewarding him with two things his son wanted. He's taking him to Little Rock, Ark., in April to play in the national elementary chess championship tourney.

"And I'll show you how to run titles," he told his son. The elder Fleming is a lawyer. Elliott had been bugging his dad to teach him how to do property title searches on a computer.

It was a good weekend for Lexington students. Boris Kaidanov (Community Montessori) was the primary (K-3) state champ and Joseph Bell,

Herald-Leader/David Perry

Somewhere in the crowded paddock at Keeneland (Oct. 10, 1998), Don Edwards' character Buffy Bleugrazz and her cousin, Barbara Jean Birdwhistle, must be looking at other people to see what they're wearing and who they're with — or maybe it's the other way around?

Don Edwards' wife, Elaine Edwards, was the inspiration for his character, Buffy Bleugrazz, "our pseudonymous social arbiter" for all matters of fashion and society, especially in the Keeneland clubhouse.

Don Edwards personal photo

Don Edwards stands still as cyclist Ricardo Flores rides his motorcycle through the Death Dome of the Fearless Flores Circus, part of the 1998 Bluegrass Fair.

Herald-Leader/Mark Cornelison

Herald-Leader/David Perry

A morning workout at Lexington's fabled Calumet Farm.

Herald-Leader file photo

Gov. A.B. "Happy" Chandler, and his wife
Mildred — "Mama" he always called her —
singing on the campaign trail in 1938.

Herald-Leader file photo

Three Kentucky icons: University of Kentucky basketball coach Adolph Rupp, U.S. Senator Wendell Ford and Kentucky Fried Chicken's global ambassador, Col. Harland Sanders.

When actress Zsa Zsa Gabor came to Lexington as a Derby guest, she had lost count of her many husbands; Don Edwards had done his research and helped her remember.

Herald-Leader file photo

To Don,
You are great
Love!
Terry Moore

One of Don Edwards' favorite photos is this one actress Terry Moore sent the Herald-Leader columnist after he interviewed her; her escort is actor James Dean.

Kentucky native Tommy Kirk attained early fame as an actor in Walt Disney films, until Disney found out that Kirk was gay and kicked him out of the corporation.
Herald-Leader file photo

Rupp Arena draws thousands to downtown Lexington every year, but, yes, downtown had a life long before the arena opened in 1976.

Rick Pitino restored and transformed the University of Kentucky's basketball tradition, paving the way for UK's first black head basketball coach, Tubby Smith, below, a former Pitino assistant. Both men guided UK to NCAA championships.

Few events in the Bluegrass have been more celebrated than the Derby Eve parties at Hamburg Place, hosted by Anita Madden, right, and her husband, Preston Madden. Guests at the 1982 party included New Yorkers Nancy Axthelm, left, and Bonnie Axthelm, center, the sisters of sports writer Pete Axthelm, a frequent visitor to Lexington and a good friend of the Maddens and Don Edwards.

Rock 'n' roll star "Bo" Diddley evoked lots of memories when he came to play at a private party in Lexington.

The heart of downtown Lexington in the old days, where Main Street intersected with Limestone, right.

Lee Cummings, a relative of Col. Harland Sanders, knew the Colonel's secret recipe and relied on it to create Lee's Famous Recipe Fried Chicken. Many customers said that Lee's chicken tasted better than the Colonel's.

Kentucky native **Robert Penn Warren** enjoyed a hearty laugh during his interview with Don Edwards. Warren was the nation's poet laureate and a three-time winner of the Pulitzer Prize — and the only person to win for both fiction (once) and poetry (twice).

Herald-Leader file photo

Kentucky author **Walter Tevis** wrote such novels as *The Hustler* and *The Man Who Fell to Earth*, both of which became popular Hollywood movies.

Herald-Leader
file photo

Don Edwards covered the student demonstrations on the University of Kentucky campus in May 1970, when protesters were tear-gassed.

Don Pratt, acting according to his conscience, burned his draft card during the Vietnam War and went to prison. He later ran the popular neighborhood store, Woodland Grocery, until he closed it in 1998. But Pratt remained outspoken on political issues.

Three women — Louise Smith, Elaine Thomas and Mona Stafford — told Don Edwards how they saw a UFO and were abducted by aliens in 1976.

The Canary Cottage was a popular downtown restaurant for decades. When it closed in 1951, Lexington lost another landmark in the slow but unending decline of its old business district in the heart of the city.

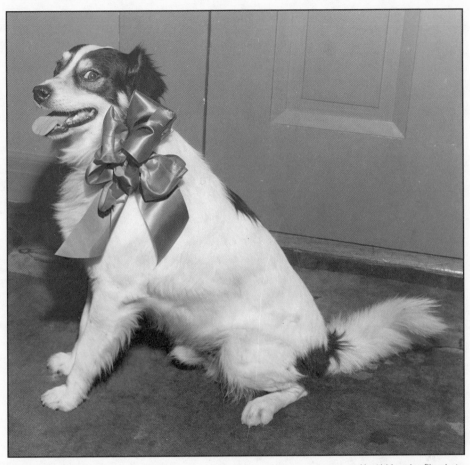

Smiley Pete, the town dog was freshly bathed and dressed up for a big downtown parade. He flashed his trademark smile that endeared him to Lexingtonians.

It is a classic Bluegrass moment: On a gorgeous day at Keeneland, two swift thoroughbreds charge to the finish, each seeking its moment of glory in the winner's circle. This scene, and so many others like it, symbolize the important role thoroughbred racing plays in Kentucky culture.

Satish Goud (both of Lexington Traditional Middle School) and Adam Goldstein (Henry Clay High School ninth- grader) shared the junior high crown with Serger Shchukin, a player from Louisville. Joshua Price of Murray and John Foster of Crittenden County shared the high school crown.

Because Elliott and I have worked at chess together for two years, sometimes parents of other players ask me: "What's Elliott's secret?"

I always lean over and tell them confidentially: "You have to be your pieces."

Friday, March 2, 1990

HOW TO REFORM EDUCATION — ACCORDING TO THE OLD SCHOOL

I don't feel at all out of touch with the new wave of educational reform in Kentucky.

Believe it or not, that stuff already was in the public school system when I was a kid.

"Reform" simply means to reshape.

Hardly a day went by in my school without the principal threatening to reshape some eighth-grader's skull.

"If you don't keep quiet, I'll put a pump-knot on your head," the principal would say.

(I don't know why a lump on the head was called a pump-knot in those days. People don't still say that, do they?)

We even had pre-kindergarten science training. It consisted of pouring a pack of salted peanuts into an RC Cola and shaking it up to see what happened.

Naturally, we all loved school. I am sure that many of my old classmates still diagram sentences in their spare time just for the fun of it.

Here are some of the modern educational concepts that were in use back then, along with the ways teachers communicated them to students:

No state-established curriculum — "You kids go out and play. You've given me a sick headache."

Vocational rehabilitation — "You aren't getting out of shop class until you learn how to make an ashtray."

Performance-based measure of ability — "We're going to have to burn the schoolhouse down to get you out of the third grade."

State-established improvement plans — "If you sell enough of these candy bars, we can all take a trip to Frankfort and see the Capitol."

Uniform performance standard — "About the only thing you're going to be good for is to join the Army."

Abolition of grade levels — "I don't know where we're going to put you. Can't you even do fractions?"

Creative student involvement — "Anybody who wants to learn more about music, raise your hand. OK, you six come help me move the piano."

Alternative certification — "Your regular teacher's sick today, so I'm substituting. I got somebody else to take my place at the gas station."

Clearly defined academic goals — "If I catch anybody cheating, I'm going to flunk all of you."

Skill measurement — "As big as you are, you ought to know not to put your finger in a pencil sharpener."

Specialized instruction — "Don't ask why. Just do it!"

Bonuses for good schools — "If you don't tear this place down, we might let you out a day early this year."

Help for bad schools —"Free milk today."

Socialization enhancement — "Get your finger out of your ear."

Decentralized decision making — "You heard what I said — shut up and read."

Saturday, June 10, 1995

CONFUSED BY KERA? TRY THIS HOME TEST

If you have followed the controversy about the Kentucky Education Reform Act, maybe you have wondered how many other states could have this much fun for only a billion dollars.

Some parents are worried that their kids are not learning enough and demand to know why the KERA test scores are so confusing.

Relax, parents. Now there's a way that you test your own kids and find out whether they've learned what they need to know to be a successful Kentuckian.

I. Thinking Skills Section:

1. How far can a bear go into the woods?

 (Correct answer: Halfway. After that, the bear is going OUT of the woods.)

II. Math Section:

1. How many square feet are in a basketball court?

(Correct answer: If you don't have lower-arena seats, what difference does it make?)

III. Geography Section:

1. In a dry county, how far is it to a bootlegger's house?

(Correct answer: Five miles or less in any direction.)

IV. Technology Section:

1. Student must demonstrate proficiency in one of the following:

(a) Personal computer.

(b) Pocket calculator.

(c) Fuzzbuster radar detector.

V. Social Studies Section:)

1. If you mix 100 proof bourbon and 90 proof bourbon, do you get 190 proof bourbon?

(Correct answer: No, stupid.)

Well, those are the basics. If the kid can't get past the Thinking Skills Section, better put him or her in private school.

For 200 years in Kentucky, nobody worried that much about test scores.

Other types of testing were used to evaluate children.

There was the Precipitation Evacuation Test. It was quite brief. It consisted of one question:

"Does the kid know enough to come in out of the rain?"

There was the Collision Apperception Test. It was equally brief. The question was:

"Does the kid have knocking-around sense?"

And there was the Cerebral Quantitative Test:

"Does the kid have even half a brain?"

All of these tests were conducted at home by one's family and friends at no expense to the taxpayers. Often they were followed by the Unpleasant Descriptive Commentary:

"I swear, if you HAD a brain, it'd rattle."

The odd thing is that people who were raised under these deplorable conditions later grew up to drive trucks and win Nobel prizes and do a million other things — including teaching others.

Perhaps it is because they knew they had to learn SOMETHING or they were in big trouble. As children, when they came home in the afternoon after loitering somewhere else as long as possible, they invariably had to face a serious question:

"What did you learn in school today?"

Unacceptable answers were:
(a) "Nothing."
(b) "I don't know."
(c) "I can't remember."

It was a sort of daily pre-KERA test administered by parents and guardians to reassure themselves that they were getting something in return for their taxes.

And so here we are, all these years later, with educators waving tests and, in effect, saying: "Yes! The kids have learned something! Look — I can prove it with these test scores!"

But do they know how far a bear can go into the woods?

Thursday, December 22, 1994

STATE'S POOR CHILDREN DESERVE A CHANCE

His parents were immigrants who spoke a foreign language and were members of a minority religious sect. They came to the United States in search of a better life.

He could speak little English when he started school. His father died when he was a child. He was raised in a home of six children headed by his mother and his oldest brother, who had quit school to work and help the family.

There was not much money in the house. As he grew up, he took on any unskilled labor he could find. At one time, he was a janitor.

It doesn't sound like much of a resume, does it? And yet, the building that holds the most people in downtown Lexington is named in his honor.

It's called Rupp Arena.

In a new book, *Adolph Rupp — Kentucky's Basketball Baron*, author Russell Rice recounts Rupp's early life in Kansas and reminds us that the most established public figure can spring from a humble beginning.

That used to be one of America's great lessons. The best-known native Kentuckian of the 19th century, Abraham Lincoln, was another example of it. In a state with many poor children, few had a poorer beginning than he.

These things are worth thinking about this week. With one ear, we hear the holiday message of peace and good will; with the other, we hear harsh political debates about illegal immigrants and welfare reform.

Some adults might not deserve a third, fourth or fifth chance, but there is no child that doesn't deserve a first chance.

One of the things that has changed the most in Lexington in recent years is the variety of its children. In my neighborhood, I see more kids from other parts of the world than ever before.

In the past year, just by chance, I have met schoolchildren from Mexico, Haiti, Panama, the Philippines, India, Japan, China, Korea, Russia and the former Yugoslavia.

Most of them had, like Adolph Rupp's family, three things in common: a family that stuck together, a family that believed in hard work and a family that knew the value of education.

Because of that, these children from other countries were getting a better start in life in Lexington than many poverty-ridden Kentucky kids whose families have been in the state for generations.

Behind the clubhouse and the mint juleps of the cultivated Kentucky image is an ugly, shameful backside of the track — the number of children living in poverty in this so-called commonwealth. Some estimates place that number as high as 25 percent.

It is interesting to see how many hearts open up to charity during the holiday season, then close down and ignore the problem the rest of the year.

Christmas has a great serve, but not much of a follow-through.

Kentuckians love their sentimental traditions more than their actual history. Child poverty in this state is as old and well established as any of those traditions. If future historians judge Kentucky by the life it continues to offer its low-income children, heaven knows what the history books will say about us.

The idea that taking good care of young people helps take care of the future is something worth remembering every time there's a basketball game in Rupp Arena.

After all, you never know which child might grow up to be a person after whom an arena is named.

Monday, September 16, 1985

LANDMARKS OF YOUTH IN CORBIN GONE

CORBIN— Growing up here in the 1940s, you learned early that trains were like highways — the even-numbered ones ran east and west; the odd, north and south.

It was a railroad town. And in those soft summer evenings of childhood when you played kick-the-can among the shadowy trees lining Master Street, you might hear a locomotive whistle far in the distance, and some railroad man sitting in a porch swing would unsnap the case on his pocket watch and say:

"Number 37's on time tonight."

The town was bisected by Louisville & Nashville Railroad tracks atop a concrete underpass. At the YMCA on Depot Street near the L&N station, railroaders showered the cinders and coal dust out of their hair, then sat outside and played checkers and dominoes. Even the local Chamber of Commerce was housed in an L&N caboose that had been brought downtown on a temporary spur of track.

The town, scattered over bits of three counties — Knox, Laurel and Whitley, but not the county seat of any of the three — had sprung up alongside those steel rails and wooden crossties. In 1939, the *WPA Writers Guide to Kentucky* described it this way:

"Corbin (1,046 altitude; 8,026 population), a busy railroad center in a level part of the Cumberland Plateau, is surrounded by a generally mountainous area with large tracts of timber and coal. ... In 1775, when Daniel Boone cut his trace, which later became a part of the Wilderness Road into Kentucky, he turned north at this place.

"The land on which the town stands was granted to Alex McClardy, one of Boone's associates, in 1798, but remained little more than a wilderness until 1883 when the main line of the L&N Railroad was built."

By the 20th century, the highways were following the railroad. U.S. 25 went straight down Corbin's Main Street. Every vehicle going south came through town, from trucks to carloads of tourists, who were bemused by the big sign at the Wilbur Hotel advertising pheasant under glass for $1.25.

On the edge of town was Harland Sanders' restaurant and motel. Sanders, an Indiana native who could swear like a sailor one minute and quote Scripture the next, was a squinty-eyed, round-faced man with dark hair who had scratched out a living in southeastern Kentucky at a variety of trades, everything from selling plumbing supplies to doing a bit of bootlegging.

In Corbin, he gradually had built a roadside gas station into a restaurant that was a popular after-church Sunday dinner place, known for its fried chicken and cream gravy.

The town must have been smaller in those days, but it seemed more crowded — particularly on Saturday when country people came in for shopping and entertainment. There would be blackberry peddlers, banjo players passing the hat, street-corner preachers warning of the wrath of God, old men swapping knives, women wearing sunbonnets, bearded patriarchs of a religious sect called the House of David, and children lining up to buy tickets at the two Main Street movie theaters, the Hippodrome and the Viv.

Much of that old Corbin is gone now. The whistle of steam engines gave way long ago to the blare of diesel horns. The L&N became part of Seaboard System Railroads.

Colonel Sanders became world famous for his Kentucky Fried Chicken; a state historical marker that terms him "Kentucky's Most Famous Citizen" stands by a KFC restaurant on the site of Sanders' old motel.

The interstate highway bypassed U.S. 25. Gone are the Wilbur and Arden hotels, the downtown movie houses. Closer to the spirit of the new Corbin is the Holiday Inn next to Interstate 75 and the sprawling Trademart Shopping Center on the edge of town with its Cinema 4, fast-food restaurants, videotape and waterbed stores.

The 1980 census listed Corbin with 8,075 population, almost the same as the 1939 figure, but the tri-county area of Knox, Laurel and Whitley has grown to more than 100,000 and Corbin is the area's largest town.

Because it was not a county seat and had no courthouse, Corbin was always its own reference point. When an annual town festival was founded, Corbin spelled its own name backward and called it the Nibroc Festival.

Some things about the place haven't changed. It's still a town where people sitting on front porches wave at you as you drive by, and the most exciting thing on Friday night is the high school football game.

People still disagree over legalizing alcoholic beverages. "Vote Whitley County Wet Or Tax The Churches," reads an anonymous scrawl on a wall near a popular restaurant. Corbin has always had its bootleggers; in the old days, the best-known was a man called "Buggytop."

Walking on the east side of town, you remember it as the part of Corbin that always flooded when Lynn Camp Creek overran its banks.

The flood would come suddenly, sometimes in the middle of the night. Residents would put their furniture up on sawhorses and abandon their houses; the muddy water once rushed so high that it reached the crossbar of the goal posts on the football field where the Corbin High Redhounds played, and boats would rescue stranded people from their own rooftops.

With those and other memories in mind, you walk the east side, from a slight rise on Ford Avenue that the kids once called "Sugar Hill" down to Master Street, looking for some trace of yourself.

Most of the landmarks of your youth have disappeared: Rose's Cafe,

King's Corner, Strickland's Grocery. Gone, too, are those human landmarks; an old man called "Squirrel Doc," who collected junk in a pushcart; and Joe, a neighborhood character who invariably yelled "You married yet? Got an old sweater?" at passers-by, but whose addled brain could remember ancient ball game scores and where everybody was buried in Pine Hill Cemetery.

What it comes down to is that you look for another kind of landmark, some touchstone from your past; something that you had thought would always be there.

At the rear of East Ward School, on the edge of the playground where you once shot marbles and played mumbletypeg, was a big beech tree clinging to the eroded bank of a stream small enough to jump across and shallow enough to catch crawdads in.

The tree was a sort of living record of the boys who went to school at East Ward. Its bark was covered with names and initials carved with Barlow pocketknives; at the highest reaches were those that had gone before you — names such as Jack "Bat" Vermillion and Mickey Root — and below were the names of you and some of your contemporaries of 1954: Glenn Sasser, Jerry Pace, Vernon Wilder, A.B. McCowan, Ronnie Rose, Tony Lanham, Terry Smith.

You stand there one day more than 30 years later and see that the tree is gone now, its names existing only in memory, and you think of some of the things people have said about home:

Home, sweet home. There's no place like home. You can't go home again. Home is where they have to take you in. Home is where you hang your hat.

But home is where you hang your heart, too. And like Boone did in 1775, you "turn north at this place," driving away, going back to the home you now have, leaving the past to dream its own dreams and bury its own dead.

Don Edwards left Corbin in 1958.

JUST SOME THOUGHTS

In the life of a columnist, the mind goes in many directions — sometimes all at once. One day it arrives at humor when it examines the four basic food groups. On another day, it turns toward nostalgia — memories of harmless Halloween pranks and the summers of youth. On still other days, the mind becomes annoyed and even angry — over the need for better schools and the difficulties of reform. The mind can be frightened by UFOs — or an illness that is all-too-real. Then, as on other days, the columnist is grateful for friends and his sense of hope renewed. In his heart, as in his mind, he wants to go "where the music of life is playing and try to dance again."

Wednesday, October 19, 1988

ENGLISH ISN'T EASY FOR THE TYPICAL KENTUCKIAN

Because he received so much publicity this year, that mythical typical Kentuckian named Bubba has become a celebrity.

Everybody wants to ask his opinion on who's going to win the presidential race, the World Series, the Robin Givens-Mike Tyson divorce case and next year's Kentucky Derby.

We, too, wished to speak with Bubba.

In 1984, the Kentucky General Assembly enacted a new section of Chapter 2 of the Kentucky Revised Statutes. It read: "English is designated as the official state language of Kentucky." That's why we went looking for Bubba.

We wanted to ask Bubba how four years of speaking the official state language had changed his life.

We found him leaning against a pickup and listening to his Walkman.

"Well," he said, taking off the earphones, "I'm plumb tuckered out. It ain't been easy — uh, pardon me, I mean to say I'm greatly fatigued and it has been somewhat difficult making the adjustment to a new language."

"Are there any parts of the old language that you especially miss?" we asked.

"As a matter of fact, there are," he said. "I particularly miss 'rat cheer,' 'far place' and 'fur piece.'

"However, through diligent practice, I have learned to say 'right here,' 'fireplace' and 'a long distance' instead."

"How about 'mep yew' and 'yello' — any difficulty with those?" "No, no. Not having been employed in a service industry, 'may I help you' was never a problem with me.

"And even before the new official language took effect, I never answered the telephone with 'hello' — I simply said: 'Bubba's residence.'"

"And tell us about eliminating the long 'i'," we said. "Is that going well?"

"Quite well, thank you," he replied. "I learned the short 'i' by repeating, 'It's a nice night for a knife fight tonight' until I mastered it.

"Also, I now accentuate the second, rather than the first, syllable of words such as 'finance' and 'insurance.'"

We asked Bubba about the tape in his Walkman.

"Before 1984," he said, "I would play my banjer — excuse me, I mean to say my banjo — and sing: 'Somebody stole my ol' hound dog, I wisht they'd bring him back. He chased big hawgs through the fence and little 'uns through the crack.'

"Now I listen to New Age music instead. It is rather soothing and I listen to it a right smart time — excuse me, I mean to say I listen to it quite frequently."

"Would you agree," we asked, "that it's amazing what the General Assembly can do to change a typical Kentuckian's life?"

"Yes, buddy," he said. "I reckon I would."

Wednesday, April 10, 1991

THE FOUR FOOD GROUPS

This is so embarrassing.

There is a big national fight about kicking meat and milk out of the four basic food groups.

The reason I'm embarrassed is that it turns out I didn't even know the four basic food groups.

I thought they were (1) corn Bugles, (2) Kool-Aid, (3) Pop-Tarts and (4) Spaghetti-Os.

That is from a cosmopolitan perspective, of course.

Speaking regionally, I thought the four Central Kentucky food groups were (1) country ham, (2) cheese grits, (3) corn pudding and (4) Ale-8-1.

Naturally, not everybody agrees with that.

Some say the four Central Kentucky food groups are: (1) beaten biscuits, (2) bourbon balls, (3) High Bridge Spring Water and (4) Laura's Lean Beef.

Others are convinced the four Lexington food groups are (1) McDonald's (2) Pizza Hut, (3) Kentucky Fried Chicken and (4) Long John Silver's.

And some insist there are only two basic Lexington food groups: (1) White Castle hamburgers and (2) Blue Monday candy bars.

I don't know why there is such wide disagreement about this.

There was a time when people began life with the same basic two food groups: (1) milk and (2) formula.

Then horrible stuff happened and the basic four food groups became: (1) strained meat, (2) strained vegetables, (3) strained cereal and (4) things you pick up off the floor.

Well, we get older and wiser.

There was a time in my life when the basic four food groups were (1) bubble gum, (2) jelly on white bread, (3) Cracker Jack and (4) any cola with a bag of peanuts dumped into it.

Then I became a teen-ager and suddenly knew everything.

Immediately I recognized that the basic food groups were: (1) cheeseburgers, (2) chocolate shakes (3) fries and (4) pizza.

I had friends who were raised in the country. They told me I was wrong.

They said the four basic food groups were: (1) soup beans, (2) corn bread (3) ham meat and (4) home fries.

(Note: They never said just "ham." They always said "ham meat." If any of them had said just "ham," the others would have known he'd been hanging out in town too much, probably at the pool hall.)

Writing this has made me hungry. Pardon me while I devour a head of Bibb lettuce.

And I can tell you one thing.

I am resisting the final four basic food groups: (1) glucose, (2) Demerol, (3) get-well cards and (4) a six-figure bill.

Saturday, November 29, 1997

FAT IS WHERE YOU FIND IT

It was Mark Twain who said there are three kinds of lies — "lies, damned lies and statistics." The worst Kentucky stat this time of year is the obesity number. The hog-out holiday season just began two days ago.

It won't end until New Year's Eve. By then, lots of people will be 20 pounds heavier and whacked out of their minds.

According to public health studies, nearly 30 percent of Kentuckians are overweight.

That can't be right. When you go to a mall doesn't it seem more like 90 percent? Besides, not everybody in Kentucky is a Kentuckian.

For instance, the obesity researchers might be doing their field work on weekends and counting a lot of obese people from West Virginia who come to Kentucky for the thrill of shopping at a different Wal-Mart.

Or maybe researchers are mistakenly counting the same people over and over.

It would be easy to do because they're all wearing jeans and panda bear shirts and look exactly alike.

Besides, it's difficult to determine the exact bodyweight of Kentuckians.

Some of them weigh more because they're carrying concealed deadly weapons.

Kentucky is the kind of place where kids say, "Mommy, mommy, can I have some Slimfast?" and the answer is: "Shut up and eat your gravy."

If you were born in Kentucky, take this quick test: As a baby, the first two words you learned to say were: (a) "Go, Blue!" (b) "Sausage biscuit." (c) "Moon Pie."

If you wondered why there wasn't a choice called (d) all of the above, you might have a culturally determined food pattern that is detrimental to your health.

Fortunately, there was great health news this week.

The FDA has approved a new diet drug called Meridia. It might increase blood pressure and is so addictive that the DEA is expected to regulate it.

Isn't that wonderful? That way, you can go to the office for a checkup and your doctor can tell you: "The good news is: You've lost 20 pounds. The bad news is: You've had a stroke and a federal grand jury subpoenaed your prescriptions."

We should remember that obesity is relative to location.

For instance, you can feel like you're overweight anywhere in the world.

But if you're in the Bluegrass State, the critical question is: Are you overweight for a Kentuckian? If you can still get into two seats at Rupp Arena, you are not overweight for a Kentuckian.

If a country-fried steak seems like an appetizer, you are not overweight for a Kentuckian.

If your friends won't offer you a ride "cause our truck bed has weak shocks," you are not overweight for a Kentuckian.

So how do you know when you have a weight problem in our state? Like all great mystical things in Kentucky, the answer is somehow connected to horses.

If you go to the racetrack, lean on the rail and the rail collapses, well Nothing too drastic. Particularly this time of year.

How about just trimming an eighth of an inch of fat off the country ham?

Monday, December 16, 1991

INMATES' LAST MEALS ARE FOOD FOR THOUGHT

This is about another tribute to one of our state inventions. Every couple of years, I receive from jolly old England one of the most macabre trivia books around.

It is called Murder Update and it keeps track of homicide cases and executions around the world.

It is full of strange facts.

For instance, did you know that a citizen of China can get the death penalty for showing pornographic material?

Or that in Pakistan you can be hanged for defiling the name of the prophet Mohammed?

Or had you heard of Saeed Al Sayaf, the official executioner of Saudi Arabia, who has chopped off more than 600 heads with a sword? (All were men; because of religious reasons, the executioner does not believe in removing any part of the covering on the upper part of a woman's body. He does not behead women. He shoots them.)

OK, why am I writing about such a depressing subject? One of the things that Murder Update keeps track of is the choice of last meals of condemned prisoners in the United States.

Like the old question about which book would you want to have on a desert island, I have often pondered what I would choose for a last meal. Sorry, but I just can't seem to resist having a morbid curiosity about the last meals that others chose.

If you don't want to know this stuff, now's the time to switch over to the comics page and read "Nancy" or something.

In 1988-90, the favorite choices for last meals on Death Rows in the United States were:

1. Hamburger and fries.
2. Pizza.
3. Fast-food chicken.
4. Steak (T-bone was the most popular cut).
5. Seafood platter.

The favorite last drinks were cola and iced tea. (Alcoholic beverages aren't allowed, so what did you expect?)

The favorite salad dressing was bleu cheese. Favorite desserts were ice cream and pie. Of fast-food chicken ordered for last meals on Death Rows, the most popular was:

Kentucky Fried Chicken.

KFC probably won't want to mention this in its ads, but what could be a more genuine compliment?

The survey did not say which style of KFC was the favorite, but I'm betting on original recipe. There are times when cholesterol just doesn't matter.

Tuesday, May 17, 1994

ONCE A COLONEL, ALWAYS A COLONEL

Alas, most of us are destined to play only small roles in history.

"I am not Prince Hamlet, nor was meant to be," wrote T.S. Eliot.

"Am an attendant lord, one that will do

"To swell a progress, start a scene or two ..."

Ah, so true. Mere attendants to fame, most of us.

And so, last week while I was on vacation, my one attendant contribution to Kentucky cultural history was lost — lost in a larger drama played out in a death chamber in Illinois while the world watched.

Was John Wayne Gacy the only famous American serial killer who was also a Kentucky Colonel?

And what a colonel he was — Gacy was so proud of his Kentucky Colonel's commission that he kept it on the wall of his cell on Death Row.

"Yes, suh, Colonel Gacy, suh," I used to imagine the other Death Row inmates saying while sipping mint juleps at the annual prison Derby party.

"Tell us, colonel — how is it that you-all had about 30 dead bodies buried under y'all's house?"

Gacy had been commissioned a Kentucky Colonel in happier days, when he managed a KFC restaurant in the Midwest.

It must have meant a lot to him. So many people had seen his colonel's certificate that somebody finally called me and asked: "Is this creep really a Kentucky Colonel?"

One hot day in July 1987 when I had nothing better to do, I decided to find out.

I called the Honorable Order of Kentucky Colonels way out west (in Louisville) and spoke with Dorothy Smith, secretary and keeper of the great seal.

"Yes, we have a Colonel John W. Gacy," she said. "The address is in Chicago."

"Do you know who Colonel Gacy is?"

"No, but if he's one of our colonels, I'm sure he's probably a nice person."

"Well, he's the Chicago serial killer who murdered 33 people and buried most of them under his home."

"He's going off the rolls right now," she said firmly. "We're very proud of our members and I'm sorry we had a mass murderer among them. But that's human nature — we're bound to have some bad apples."

And yes, there it is, my contribution to cultural history: It was I who got John Wayne Gacy kicked off the membership list of the Honorable Order of Kentucky Colonels.

Unfortunately, he was still a Kentucky Colonel.

"You can never take their colonelcy away from them," Smith said. "That was given by the governor."

But by being kicked off the members' list, Gacy joined such luminaries as Richard Nixon and Waldo Wecker.

You probably don't remember Colonel Waldo. He was kicked off the list in 1980 amid a scandal.

It turned out that Colonel Waldo was a sheep dog that somebody had gotten a colonel's commission for as a joke. The other colonels weren't amused.

I thought about all this last week when Gacy was executed. He has only been gone a week and already I don't miss him.

But did you notice what Gacy ordered for his last meal?

Yep, the menu included fried chicken.

I'm telling you — once a colonel, always a colonel.

Saturday, May 27, 1995

AH, THE SIGNS OF SUMMER: DRIVE-INS, CAR COOKING

There was a time when summer began on Memorial Day and ended on Labor Day.

You knew it was really summer when people took the awnings out of the garage and put them on the house.

And you knew it was really summer when you flew a June bug on a string or caught a jar full of lightning bugs to use as a "headlight" for your bicycle.

It was summer when movie theaters put up banners that said: COME

IN — IT'S COOL INSIDE.

It was summer when the swimming pools opened. And when Japanese lanterns were strung in trees and people danced to band music on pavilions.

You knew it was summer when radio stations had "treasure hunts" and broadcast clues that had you chasing all over town to try to find a hidden envelope worth $50.

You knew it was summer when the local "passion pit" (drive-in movie) started advertising $1-a-carload night. And when people began talking about making a big trip to Coney Island at Cincinnati or Fontaine Ferry amusement park at Louisville.

And you knew it was a little bit of a crazy summer if your father decided to try car cooking — a fad designed to promote aluminum foil. Suppose you were going to drive to a family reunion and picnic on a holiday weekend.

If you were going on such a trip, you could wrap a ham heavily in foil and secure it under the hood of the family car. Halfway there, you turned the ham over onto its other side.

By the time you arrived, the heat of the engine would have cooked the ham.

Or so the theory went. For some reason, the people who insisted on trying car cooking were always dads; there is no record of any mom ever endorsing such a scheme.

It was almost summer when your school celebrated May Day with a festival and the boys performed in skits and the girls danced around the May pole and everybody brought a May basket to school.

But it was summer for sure if you fell out of a hammock. Or if you went to camp and fell out of a canoe. And it was summer for sure if you went blackberry picking and came home with chiggers.

It was definitely a summer day when peddlers went door to door selling homegrown corn and tomatoes.

It was definitely a summer night if you watched home movies on a screen in your back yard. Or played hide-and-seek or kick-the-can.

For most people, the space age began in back yards. That was where they would stand and watch Sputnik, the first satellite, go sailing across the night sky.

You knew it was summer if the bird bath was crowded. And if you could hear the clatter of a lawn mower's blades.

It was summer if you canned and pickled. It was summer if you fanned and prickled. Heat rash, talcum powder, poison ivy, Calamine lotion.

It was summer if you longed for fireworks. Big bottle rockets that would reach the sky. And sparklers and cherry bombs.

It was summer when the carnival came to town with such sideshow attractions as "Hitler's Armored Car" and "The Alligator Man." There was a time when you could ride the Tilt-a-Whirl for a nickel, but the Tunnel of Love cost a dime.

Of the many things a person might learn between Memorial Day and Labor Day, maybe that was the grand, eternal lesson of summer: Love is always more expensive than the Tilt-a-Whirl.

Tuesday, August 9, 1994

KILL CRUELTY: PRACTICE GARDENING CORRECTNESS

Last week in New Jersey, a 69-year-old man named Frank Balun used a broomstick to kill a rat that was eating his tomato plants.

Balun has been taken to court by an animal rights group that says he should have either killed the rat by lethal injection or trapped the rat and set it free in the wild.

This is no joke, folks. A hearing on the complaint is set for Aug. 24, and the case is drawing national attention.

I am glad that I live in Kentucky, where a person can defend his or her garden and still has a few more rights than a rat.

But how long will that last? What if the New Jersey case goes all the way to the U.S. Supreme Court and the majority opinion comes down on the side of the rat? There would have to be some changes in the Bluegrass state, a place where most folks think a lethal injection for a rat is something you do with a .22 rifle.

Don't wait for the worst to happen. Here, before you need it, is the Kentucky Guide to Gardening Correctness:

PROBLEM: Raccoons in your sweet corn.

OLD SOLUTION: Shotgun or dog.

NEW SOLUTION: Raccoons are famous for being fastidious and washing their food before eating it. Put a speaker in the garden and play some Nirvana grunge music. The raccoons will leave immediately.

PROBLEM: Slugs on your tomatoes.

OLD SOLUTION: Salt the slugs and watch them die in agony. Or leave shallow pans of beer in the garden; they'll drink it until they explode.

NEW SOLUTION: Eat the whole thing. "What's for dinner tonight, dear?" "Escargot and tomato." "Yum!"

PROBLEM: Crows.

OLD SOLUTION: Scarecrow.

NEW SOLUTION: Hire an old hippie to stand in your garden and give the peace sign.

Well, you get the idea. Just keep your gardening non-confrontational.

And by the way, how do you get a rat to hold still for a lethal injection? Well, it's not easy. First you encourage the rat to relax, lie back in a comfortable chair and listen to National Public Radio. Then say: "This will only take a moment."

Hey, not everyone in New Jersey has a deficit of common sense. The board of health in the town where the rat homicide occurred — a place called Hillside — is backing up the guy who killed the rat because rats carry disease.

That's really scary because what if the guy who killed the rat had done what the animal rights people said? What if he had trapped the rat and released it into the wild — and then it bit somebody who got a disease and sued the guy for releasing a diseased rat into the wild? Even if he had killed the rat by lethal injection, he would still have had the problem of disposing of a diseased rat corpse, which has to be considered hazardous waste. In other words, it's starting to look to me as if there is no way that the guy who killed the rat can win.

He should have killed that rat in the dead of night with no eyewitnesses and dumped the body in a place where it might never be found. Isn't that what the mob does when it kills somebody in New Jersey?

If you're laughing at this, just remember that the day might come when you are led away in handcuffs because a dead 'possum was found stuck in the grille of your pickup.

As for me, I will be watching one of those old gangster movies where Humphrey Bogart says, "Take that, you dirty rat!"

Sunday, April 1, 1990

BALLYHOO ABOUT AN UNGLAMOROUS ASPECT OF THE CIRCUS

First you have to imagine a ringmaster striding up to a microphone and saying in a booming voice: "Ladies and gentlemen, girls and boys — welcome! Welcome to ... The Greatest Fertilizer on Earth!" Yes, the Ringling

Bros. and Barnum & Bailey Circus is playing Lexington this weekend.

And this is a report on the least glamorous aspect of the circus. This is about the M-word.

That is, manure. The circus generates almost as much as a political convention.

Consider the numbers.

In an average week, the animals of "The Greatest Show on Earth" eat 12 tons of hay, 1.5 tons of sweet feed and oats, 400 pounds of carrots, 350 pounds of meat, 150 loaves of bread, 70 pounds of apples, 60 pounds of oranges, 50 pounds of bananas and 30 heads of lettuce.

"We call this the pachyderm-poo giveaway," said circus promoter Scott Kane, pointing to a 5-ton dumpster of elephant and horse manure in an area behind Rupp Arena.

The circus had scheduled a free-to-the-public manure pickup at 10 a.m. yesterday. As the magic hour arrived, nobody had showed. But there was a long day ahead and Kane was hopeful.

"In Des Moines, the farmers line up for this stuff," said Pete Cimini, who works with the show's animals.

"Elephant manure is so potent it'll grow cherry tomatoes the size of softballs. But you have to let it rot four or five weeks before you can use it."

Cimini has seen some strange things.

"In Philadelphia," he said, "they had a celebrity elephant-chip-throwing tournament. They did it like a shot put.

"And in Birmingham, there's a police officer who always gets a bucket of elephant chips. He has them bronzed and gives them to his friends as paperweights."

Cimini knows some strange things.

"Let me tell you a secret," he said. "Tiger manure. Don't put it on the garden, put it around the garden. It's better than a scarecrow.

"Rabbits, raccoons — they get a whiff of tiger and they won't come near the place again."

Nobody is ever interested in camel and llama manure, Cimini said, "because it looks like Milk Duds and Raisinettes." Meanwhile, inside a big, blue tent stood 22 elephants, with wheelbarrows and shovels behind them at strategic intervals.

"They're always producing," Cimini said. "If nobody wants it, we just have it hauled away."

After I wrote this column, some people said, "Yuck — why not write about something else?"

"What?" I said. "And give up show business?"

Thursday, March 20, 1997

FAUX BOY: FIDO FITS IN WITH OTHER FAKE STUDS

When I first heard about this (or should I say these?), I couldn't believe it. So I called a veterinarian and asked.

"It's true" said Mike Bruestle of the Romany Road Animal Clinic. "They're called Neuticles."

Neuticles are prosthetic testicles for male dogs that have been neutered.

"Ideally, you replace the real ones with the Neuticles when you do the neutering," Bruestle said.

"But they can be ordered and put back in later."

Why would anybody pay to have a dog neutered and then pay for fake cojones for the dog to wear? Well, not anybody would.

Women, for instance, won't.

There's no scientific study. The evidence is anecdotal.

But apparently nearly all Neuticle buyers are men. They want the dog to have implants because they feel less macho walking a neutered dog in public.

"Men are the ones who usually cringe when I recommend neutering their dogs," said Bruestle. "Their knees cling together and they start sinking to the floor.

"People correlate their animals with themselves sometimes."

On the one hand, he said, "they get tired of the dog climbing over the fence and getting out" and want to calm him down.

On the other hand, he said, they think of how the dog will look and "they want to see something hanging down there."

Faking the family jewels for canines is not a new idea, said Bruestle.

"Some unethical people were doing it years ago at dog shows." Neuticles are made of the same material as human prosthetics, he said. So are other pet prosthetics, such as artificial hips.

But the idea of Neuticles amuses many people. They find it just a little strange or maybe totally stupid.

"Some people are weird," Bruestle said.

And yet, how out of place are Neuticles in a place like Lexington? Isn't the Bluegrass, if we may coin a word, somewhat testicentric?

What other city in America has a downtown horse statue like the John Hunt Morgan statue? Every Lexington history student knows that Morgan rode a famous mare named Black Bess.

But the sculptor put him on a stallion.

And so, for generations, from brushes to spray cans, Halloween pranksters have painted the bronze equine's "boys" to call attention to them (Day-Glo orange and purple were two popular colors).

And the horse business. What do breeders talk about in the horse business? OK, second to money, what do they talk about? The center of the horse business isn't where the mares graze.

It's where the stallions stand.

The horse business is about cogliones (that's Italian for you-know-what).

They really get discussed when something goes wrong with them. A brief poem will illustrate: Cigar covered 36 mares with hardly a note of thanks, And yet he hit the headlines for merely firing blanks.

Was it serious? Ask the insurance company. It cost the insurance company $25 million (and that ain't Neuticles).

In a way, even non-equine Lexington revolves around the twin spheres. Look at the part of basketball you can't see. All "athletic supporters" are not "fans." And finally, there is the question of genuine Kentucky cuisine.

"I want to try a local dish," says the unsuspecting tourist.

"Y'all sure can," says the host. "How about some lamb fries?"

Thursday, October 6, 1994

WHICH WAY DO I TURN AT MOONEY'S GARAGE?

The great thing about driving around in Kentucky is when you stop and ask directions.

"Which way to Gooberville?" you ask.

And the answer sounds like: "Blub-glubba-blub-glub." I used to get letters from tourists complaining about the lack of road signs (or at least ones without any bullet holes) and griping about the way Kentuckians give directions to strangers.

Things are better now — but only on the interstate highways. And really, if you get lost on the interstate, you shouldn't be driving.

But things are worse on the backroads than ever before.

It is true that many of us Kentuckians are provincial. If you ask us how to get to Highway 462, we say stuff like, "Just go down there to Rufus Mooney's garage and turn left."

It does not seem to occur to us that (1) maybe not everybody knows where Mooney's garage is; and (2) anybody who does know where Mooney's garage is probably already knows how to get to 462.

But that is not the major problem on the backroads these days. I have been driving the backroads looking at autumn colors, and the major problem with directions is that hardly anybody knows anything about the backroads anymore.

On the old roads, all the places that used to be motels, gas stations, restaurants and country stores are gone. They were landmarks, and in the old days the people who worked there could give you directions.

Now the motels and gas stations and restaurants are all snuggled up to each other at interstate highway interchanges. And many of the people who work at those places commute to work on the interstate highway themselves and don't really know much about the names or numbers of those little two-lane roads just a few miles away.

If you do not have a map, you might never find what you're looking for, and a state map is not detailed enough — you need a county map.

What have interstate highways done to us? They have made it easier to zoom around to big cities all over the United States, but harder to find your way around in the country with a bunch of cows 50 miles from where you live.

And what does it mean any more to be local? We all watch the same TV shows and movies, wear the same kinds of sneakers, go to the same kinds of malls and eat the same fast food.

There used to be great wails of public dismay about the decline of geography as a school subject among young people. Tests would show that many Kentucky children couldn't figure out where Louisville or Frankfort or Covington or Paducah would be on a blank map of the state.

In recent years, the decline in reading, writing and mathematics seemed to overshadow the decline in geography. Forget about Louisville and Paducah — it would be interesting today to see how many kids could write a usable set of directions from their home to a place 5 miles away.

And after the kids take a shot at it, we ought to test the adults.

Yes, I am aware that there is an information explosion and an information superhighway and more information than ever, blah, blah, blah, blah.

But there are some things that people simply cannot learn by staring into a computer screen, and one of them is which way to turn at Mooney's garage.

Sunday, August 17, 1986

"BOOM" BRINGS BACK MEMORIES OF ANOTHER CLOSE ENCOUNTER

Pull your chair up close to the edge of the truth and I'll tell you a story.

The mysterious "boom" and bright flash in the sky over Clark County last week reminded me that nearly everybody has a UFO story.

Here's mine. It happened 10 years ago, and it remains the strangest UFO incident recorded in Central Kentucky.

I was assigned to the story and spent a couple of weeks investigating it.

When it was over, I still couldn't decide whether it was a hoax that fooled me or a distorted reality — or maybe just some wild kind of misunderstanding.

On the night of Jan. 6, 1976, three Casey County women were driving on a lonely stretch of Ky. 78 from Stanford to Liberty. They had been to dinner at a Stanford restaurant. They knew one another but were not the closest of friends. In fact, it was the first time the three of them had ever been together.

From the car windows, they saw what looked like a plane on fire about to crash. It came closer. They later described it as an oval aircraft with a bluish-white dome and red and yellow lights on its underside.

A bluish-white light came out of the bottom of the craft. Their car began shaking. They became terrified and began screaming. The car filled with a foglike substance. They lost consciousness.

An hour and 25 minutes later, they awoke. They were in the car but were eight miles farther down the road. They had severe headaches and 3-inch red marks on the backs of their necks; the marks resembled fresh burns. The car's electrical system was malfunctioning, and the paint on the hood of the car had bubbled up in several spots.

They could not account for the missing 85 minutes. They had no conscious memory of what had happened during that time. They decided that maybe they had had a UFO experience.

Eventually, the incident was studied by a man with the curious name of Leo Sprinkle, a clinical psychologist who was then the director of counseling and testing at the University of Wyoming. Sprinkle, who researches unexplained aerial phenomena as a hobby, came to Kentucky in the summer of 1976.

He hypnotized the three women in separate sessions. He also arranged for lie-detector tests to be given each of the women by a polygraph examiner who was also a Lexington police detective. And he investigated the women's backgrounds to see whether they were congenital liars or had a history of mental illness.

"This was one case I couldn't shoot down," Sprinkle told me later. "They all told the same story under hypnosis, and the polygraph report showed no indications of deception. In my opinion, it would be very difficult, if not impossible, for these women to fake their impressions. Two of them are grandmothers, they're all active churchgoers — they just aren't the kind of people who usually try to hoax you."

And the missing 85 minutes? Under hypnosis, the women told a classic close-encounter-of-the-third-kind story.

They had been taken aboard a spaceship, they said, and "put in a white room" and examined by strange creatures with huge pale-blue eyes "with scales around them, like a turtle's eyes." They talked about "a big crystal with lightning coming out of it." And one of the women said a powderlike substance was poured over her, then removed "like they were making a mold of me." It sounded like Hollywood sci-fi stuff — just the kind of story you would expect and the kind that most people wouldn't believe.

Inevitably, the national tabloids pounced on it. There was a spread in the National Enquirer. The next February, one of the women appeared, along with Sprinkle, on NBC's *Tomorrow* talk show and told the whole thing again to host Tom Snyder.

I stayed up late and watched the show. It was obvious that Snyder didn't believe the story.

Back in Kentucky, the three women became the laughingstock of their hometown. They couldn't walk down the street without somebody yelling: "Little green men! Little green men!"

Two of them moved away, one all the way to Nevada. I talked with her a couple of years later. "They don't laugh at me out here," she said. "There are lots of UFO study groups in this part of the country. I'm trying to learn about this and find out what really happened to me." I wished her luck. At the beginning, I hadn't believed the story, either.

A University of Kentucky psychology professor who had spent much of his career studying hypnosis and was nationally recognized in the field had once told me that people are so suggestible under hypnosis that they will tell you anything they think you want to hear.

And polygraph tests are not infallible. Some people can beat them. Or, as Sprinkle had admitted, if you believe it's the truth, you pass the polygraph.

"The usual example of that," he said, "is the guy in the asylum who believes he's Napoleon. Put him on a polygraph and ask him if he's Napoleon. If he says 'no,' the machine will indicate that he's lying. But that doesn't make him Napoleon."

I spent a lot of hours talking to those women and listening to the tapes of what they had said under hypnosis. If they were lying — and I don't think they were — they could give Meryl Streep a run for her money in the acting business.

And so that's how it ended. I believed their emotions were genuine, but I still didn't believe their story. The evidence just wasn't strong enough.

But I did believe that something happened to — or among — those three women on that January night in 1976.

Something very strange indeed. But I have no idea what it was.

That's the end of my UFO story. Now let's hear yours.

Monday, May 7, 1990

WITNESS TO HISTORY AT UK RECALLS
WHOOSH AS RIOT CLUB MISSED HEAD

History is a kind of mirror. You look into it and see some things clearly, some murkily and some not at all.

Twenty years ago, I was a witness to a bit of history. I was a reporter covering a University of Kentucky Board of Trustees meeting.

"We are proud we've had no violence at UK," said board vice chairman Albert G. Clay, who was presiding over the meeting.

Less than an hour later, a trustee had punched a student who had grabbed at his face, and UK police were swinging riot clubs, hitting bodies as if they were pounding meat.

That night, the Air Force ROTC building was burned, and a day later Kentucky National Guard troops were on campus.

One of those riot clubs missed my head by a few inches. I can still remember the whoosh it made as it went past.

That was how the Vietnam War and the Kent State shootings came home to UK the first week in May 1970.

As one who was there taking notes when the violence began, I hope a couple of things will be remembered:

One is that it all might — just might — have been prevented.

Most of the 16,000 students on campus simply were trying to get through final exams that week and go home for the summer.

The war protesters wanted the UK board meeting moved to Memorial Coliseum so everyone could attend and be heard.

The board wouldn't do that because "it was not desirable to vacate the board room at this time," Clay said.

When the protesters couldn't get a dialogue, they settled for a confrontation. And it was an angry, ugly one — with clenched fists and shouted curses.

If both sides had gone to the coliseum and talked and listened to each other with mutual respect — even if it had taken all day and half the night — at least there would have been a chance for something better than arson and soldiers and tear gas.

Another thing I remember is one person who did come out after the board meeting and sat down and talked with the students.

That was Otis Singletary, the UK president. "It was a great mistake," he said of the Cambodian invasion, which set off the protests at Kent State.

Earlier that day, Singletary had ordered — on his own — the UK flag flown at half staff and the names of the four slain Kent State students placed at the flagpole.

Like college and university presidents across the country, he was trying to hold his school together.

By then, probably nothing could have stopped the storm.

And all these years later, if the turmoil is worth remembering, then so is the need for generations to care about one another.

Saturday, July 25, 1998

INVISIBLE HEIGHTS

It was odd this week to see the name of Speigle Heights in the Sunday edition of *The New York Times Magazine*.

It was odd — and so much against all odds — to think of millions of people having a reason to read anything about Speigle Heights.

The Heights is a tiny, nearly invisible neighborhood in Lexington, a scattering of little houses on Speigle Hill that overlooks railroad tracks below.

It's roughly between West High Street and Manchester Street.

You could know Lexington a long time and not know the Heights. You might never find it if you weren't looking for it.

Most people here have no idea where it is. At least, most white people.

The Heights is a black neighborhood, off the beaten path. In distance, it's hardly more than a stone's throw down Robertson Street from Bob Mickler's, a West High Street store that sells fine English riding apparel and tack.

In psychic distance, it's more like a world away.

The Heights was mentioned in the *Times* magazine this past Sunday in an article by Peter Manso, writing about Lexington novelist Gayl Jones.

Jones was involved in a much-publicized police standoff in another part of Lexington in February. It ended with the suicide of her husband, Bob Higgins.

Here is the context in which the Heights was mentioned:

"(Born in 1949)," Manso wrote, "Gayl grew up in a cramped, dilapidated house with no indoor toilet in Speigle Heights, one of Lexington's more turbulent black neighborhoods."

And that was it. No other mention. The Heights' one sentence of recognition was over.

According to old Lexington City Directory research, Jones also lived on Florence Avenue off Georgetown Street near Douglass Park. That's a much more prosperous place than the Heights.

In the Heights this week, you could see people working on old cars in the street. On Florence, you could see at least one person driving a Mercedes Benz.

Florence Avenue is a more visible place, but I would bet that most of white Lexington couldn't tell you how to find it, either.

Both black neighborhoods are at least a half-century older than some of the shiny new subdivisions around Lexington that are already better known than the Heights and Florence Avenue ever will be.

This isn't New York. A city this size with neighborhoods that don't know of each other's existence is a divided community in a relatively small space.

It reminds you of genteel old Lexington streets lined with mansions, and just down the back alley were shacks where the people who worked in the mansions lived.

When *Newsweek* magazine wrote about Jones' new novel in February, it called the reclusive author "The Invisible Woman." Maybe part of the reason is that she grew up in a place where people continue to be invisible to one another.

Tuesday, December 6, 1994

That Crucial Christmas Sweater

I don't know when the holiday season starts at your place, but nothing happens where I am until the problem of the CCS has been solved.

The CCS is the Crucial Christmas Sweater; that is, the sweater that is actually going to be worn during the daylight hours of Dec. 25 when the family will get together.

Like many men, I have no idea what I'll be wearing tomorrow. But also like many men, the female persons to whom we are wed cannot rest until the Crucial Christmas Sweater has been acquired.

The hunt begins no later than November.

"Why can't you just wear the same sweater you wore last Christmas?"

"Because it has to be different. People always remember what you wore the year before."

The hunt can cover a great distance. It is somewhat like a safari.

"Why do we have to go to so many stores?" he asks.

"It's the only way to find the right one," she says. "You don't want one that's in EVERY store. So you have to go to a million stores to find the one that's not in every store." "Well, what kind do you want?" he says.

"It's good to get one that goes with your other stuff from the year before," she says.

"I thought you said they would remember the stuff from the year before." "Well, ALL the stuff doesn't matter," she says. "The sweater matters. Besides, if you don't get a sweater that matches your other stuff, then you have to buy a whole new outfit."

"Oh," he says.

There is a period of silence.

Finally, his bad judgment gets the better of him and he opens his mouth.

"But what kind do you want?" he asks.

"You have to strike the right balance," she says. "It can't be TOO cute. But it can't be too sophisticated, either. Because it's a family thing. You can understand that, can't you? Surely you can understand THAT."

"Yes," he lies. "I understand."

"It can't be too trendy, either," she says. "I mean, Christmas vests are good this year, but vests can be trendy."

"Yes," he says.

"I mean, if it's trendy, you CAN'T wear it again in three years when you hope people will have forgotten. If it's trendy, it'll be out in three years."

"Yes," he says.

"Pet motifs are big this year," she says. "Cats and dogs. And sweaters with little knitted doors." "Little knitted doors?" he asks.

"Yes," she says, "little knitted doors that actually open."

"Why would anybody want a door in a sweater?" he asks.

"I TOLD you," she said. "That's the motif. Like there's a row of little shops and their doors open to show little people or pets inside."

"A row of shops?"

"On the SWEATER," she says. "A row of little shops on the sweater. It's the motif. Also, antique colors are better this year than bright colors."

"Yes," he says absently. "Antique colors."

But inside, far in the corner of some lonely, recessed part of his brain, he is still trying to figure out the part about the little knitted doors.

"Mohair trim is big, too," she said. "And little jingle bells for the buttons."

"Yes," he mutters. "Little bells."

"Anyway," she says, "it's only for the daytime." "The daytime?" he asks.

"Yes," she says, "the daytime. This is just to wear in the daytime. If you wear a sweater at night, it has to be totally different. Like black and white cashmere with gold bows or seed pearls."

"Excuse me a moment," he says. And he walks through a big knitted door and closes it softly behind him.

Sunday, December 24, 1989

FOR A MOMENT, CHRISTMAS MAKES MEN BROTHERS AGAIN

Years ago, Lexington was much smaller and downtown was its heart at Christmas.

Main Street was filled with honking horns and two-way traffic. The store windows along it were elaborately decorated, including all of the town's department stores.

The sidewalks were crowded with shoppers. There were no suburban malls and no interstate highways, either.

New Circle Road was only partly completed. Everyone called it "the beltline" and it was practically out in the country.

Very few secrets are ever kept in a town of any size. And the smaller the place, the more people know about one another.

In those days, there were two brothers who could be seen downtown nearly every day.

They had a sad relationship that people who knew them often remarked about.

Their father had been killed in a railroad accident when they were children. Their mother had worked as a hotel maid and scraped together the best life she could afford for her sons.

It was a poor life in a poor neighborhood.

The older son was drafted during World War II. He sent his younger brother souvenirs from island battles in the Pacific.

When he came back from the war, he went to college on the GI Bill. He learned a profession and was successful. His name was painted in gold letters on a downtown office door.

The younger son helped break his mother's heart. He was in and out of trouble constantly.

Every attempt to help him failed. He went from the streets to jail, from jail to prison — and finally back to the streets, where he panhandled money to buy wine.

He became a hateful sight to his older brother, who would cross the street to avoid him.

For years they had been in the same town, but in different worlds. They walked the same streets, but neither would acknowledge the other's presence.

One cold Christmas Eve, not long after dark, I gave an older man I worked with a ride home. As we sat at the traffic light at Limestone and Church streets, he noticed something.

"Well, would you look at that," he said softly.

I glanced through the window of a little Italian restaurant on the corner. I didn't see anything extraordinary, just two men I didn't know having coffee at a table by the window.

One was wearing an expensive, camel-hair overcoat. The other was pitifully dressed.

"What is it?" I asked the man with me.

Then he told me the story.

It was the two brothers seated in the restaurant.

Somehow Christmas had brought them together, if only for a moment.

Thursday, August 29, 1996

REFLECTIONS ON EMERGING FROM A SHADOW

"Where have you been?" people keep asking me.

This column has been out of the newspaper for 2 1/2 months.

That's the longest I've missed doing the column since I began writing it in the late 1970s.

Like a lot of absences, mine began by going to a doctor's office. Soon a second doctor was called in to take a look at me.

Immediately I was given one of those tests where the inside of your skull gets scanned.

The technician who did the test had seemed talkative when we began. But when he was through scanning me, he didn't say anything.

"Well," I finally asked, "how did I do?"

"Good luck with it," he said.

And that was all he said.

I had that sinking feeling you get when you're watching a space shot on TV and somebody far from home says, "Houston, we have a problem."

A few minutes later, the doctor showed me the film from the test. He pointed out a cloudy area around my right eye socket.

"That shouldn't be there," he said. "That's a mass."

"Do you think it's cancer?" I said.

"It could be," he said. "We need to find out right away."

My life as a medical patient changed at that point. Up until then, I had spent years sitting in waiting rooms and reading magazines so old that Bo Jackson was on the cover.

That was because I had wanted to see doctors.

Everything is different when doctors want to see you. Suddenly I had immediate appointments to see other doctors and even a date and time for surgery.

When I did have the surgery, the weirdest thing happened. I had barely gone to sleep when I woke up and the people in the operating room told me I was fine.

"Your friends are waiting," they said. "Go on and have a good time with them."

We adjourned to a bar across the street. Everybody was laughing and buying rounds.

It was a strange crowd. Gradually, I noticed that everyone I had ever wronged in my life was there.

It was a much larger group than I had hoped for. But they told me not to worry. "We forgave you long ago," they said.

There were people I hadn't seen in years. Right away, I spotted my old friend, Jack. I hadn't seen Jack since 1960, the year he died.

Things started to go sour then. Once you recognize a dream for what it is, it becomes a letdown.

A while later, I really did wake up from the anesthetic and the doctor told me it was cancer, but not the end of the world.

After that came radiation therapy and then more surgery and another recuperation.

Anyone who has been through an extended illness and recovered can write the rest of the script: the long stretches of pain to be crossed like deserts, the bright flashes of hope, the dark moments of despair.

And finally one day you wobble back in to where the music of life is playing and try to dance again.

I was impressed with the many little courtesies patients undergoing cancer treatment show one another, even though they are of all different ethnic groups and backgrounds.

Perhaps it is easier to see the light when you're sitting in a shadow.

My wife, Elaine, began working a jigsaw puzzle of a castle left in the radiation waiting room. Gradually, others finished it as far as they could.

Nobody could completely finish it. Like life, a few pieces were missing.

KENTUCKY POLITICS

I n Kentucky, a sage once wrote, "politics (are) the damndest." What's one to say about politicians (not to mention preachers) who pack pistols? The merry antics of the "Kentucky Bubba Assembly" in Frankfort and some of its mind-boggling legislation? The belief that legalized gambling can cure all that ails the state? About governors who dream of creating their kingdoms and lieutenant governors whose ideas seem like bad dreams? Yes, in Kentucky, politics are the damndest.

Thursday, April 2, 1998

LET'S PRAY THE FLOCK DOESN'T NOD OFF

Take me back to old Kentucky,
Let me hear those pistols pop.
Let me see those politicians
with their snouts eye deep in slop.
Take me back to those blue mountains where they argue but with lead,
But you needn't rush the matter — take me back when I am dead.
— Anonymous, 19th Century

That's the kind of stuff that was written about Kentucky during the Hatfield-McCoy feud days.

My, how things have changed.

Now we write about Pistol Packin' Pete and Pistol Packin' Preachers.

State Rep. Pete Worthington, D-Ewing, on his way to the Final Four, was pounced on by airport cops in Texas last week for having a loaded .22 in his suitcase.

But he got back to Frankfort in time for the House to give final approval to a bill that lets preachers carry concealed deadly weapons in church.

Ah, Kentucky, the land we know and love. If it didn't exist, the NRA would have to invent it.

Ah, Kentucky, the land of James H. Mulligan, who wrote in 1902 that "politics (are) the damnedest" in Kentucky.

In the same poem:
Hip pockets are the thickest,
Pistol hands the slickest,
The cylinder turns quickest
In Kentucky.

Ah, Kentucky. Of thee we sing. And in 1998, here's what we sing:
Welcome to morning service and kindly take your seat,
Remember as the plate is passed: your preacher's wearing heat.

That was the rationale for the bill. It was purported to protect nervous members of the clergy carrying collection proceeds out of their churches at night.

How nervous could they be? Under the old, unconcealed gun law in Kentucky, any adult, including preachers, could carry a cannon as big as an elephant gun in plain sight on his or her hip.

If that doesn't discourage an ecclesiastical stickup, what does it take?

But just think of what fringe benefits this new law will have (besides providing Jay Leno and David Letterman with fresh material).

We can already envision a big poster in a club window that reads: "QUICK DRAW CONTEST TONITE! (SPECIAL BRACKET FOR MINISTERS)."

It might even inspire Hollywood to come out with a revival of the old *Magnum, P.I.* television show.

This time around, it could be called *Rev. Magnum, P.I.*

And best of all, it creates new jobs in our state.

Besides the usual minister of music, minister of education, etc., churches can now establish a brand new position called: minister of firearms.

Frankly, if you saw this as a routine on *Saturday Night Live*, you'd say it was too outrageous to even be believable.

But here it is and unfortunately, it's not as comical as it sounds.

When we think of what happened in West Paducah last year and Jonesboro, Ark., last week — kids shooting kids — what kind of an example does this set for young people in Kentucky?

What could legitimize guns more than having guns in church? We sympathize with the members of the clergy in Kentucky who are appalled by the whole thing.

Of all the absurdities that have been created by the Kentucky General Assembly over the years, this one seems to be in a category of its own.

Saturday Night Live, eat your heart out.

Thursday, April 4, 1996

■ On April 1, 1996, the University of Kentucky won its sixth NCAA basketball championship.

APRIL IS MONTH TO RECOGNIZE BUBBAS

Wow, what a happy time in Kentucky!

Can you imagine what life must be like in Indiana?

Bobby Knight and all those other Hoosiers are standing on the shore looking across the Ohio River to the Promised Land.

With all the joy and excitement, nearly everybody has forgotten that other important stuff is going on.

For instance, April in Kentucky is Bubba History Month.

It's the month that we celebrate the many contributions that Bubbas have made to our culture, including microwaveable Moon Pies, Conway Twitty CD offers and record-breaking crowds at NASCAR races in other states.

Or as Jeff Foxworthy might say, "If your Mama ever beat up a state cop, you just might be a Bubba."

Bubba History Month is particularly important in Kentucky because we are on the cutting edge of the whole deal.

In some places in the world, Bubbas are merely part of history. In Kentucky, Bubbas are making history.

Maybe you saw some Bubbarific behavior in Lexington Monday night if you were standing around drunk downtown or happened to get your hair parted with a thrown beer bottle in the vicinity of Euclid and Woodland avenues.

If you wondered what smashed cars and burning puddles of gasoline had to do with being happy about basketball, the answer is: nothing.

That stuff wasn't about basketball and it can't even be blamed on Joe Camel billboards.

It was the work of a few misguided individuals who are Bubba Wannabes and will one day boost the economy by providing jobs for people seeking career opportunities in the corrections field.

More substantial, however, are the goings-on in Frankfort where the Kentucky Bubba Assembly recently:

1. Tried to give itself a 50 percent pay raise.

2. Passed a concealed gun law.

3. Got rid of that pesky ethics law so that hardworking lobbyists can afford to buy as many legislators as they need.

All that junk now goes to the Gov Bub, whose philosophy is: "I ain't vetoin' nothin'."

After supporting concealed guns, the Gov Bub came out against higher speed limits for cars, trucks and dudes on Harleys.

In other words, let's save lives on the highways but a bullet in the head is OK. Even some Bubbas are confused by that one, particularly those who don't want to wear motorcycle helmets.

Some members of the Kentucky Bubba Assembly say this assembly session has been the worst in years. They are calling country radio disc jockeys and asking them to play that old song called *I'm So Depressed I Don't Whether To Commit Suicide Or Go Bowling*.

All that stuff has been stuck in the background because of the great success of the basketball team. Alas, we will now have to think about it.

Meanwhile, Bubba History Month got off to a good start nationally because of a criminal trial in Arkansas where some Bubbas who are former friends of the nation's highest-ranking Bubba are trying to stay out of prison as another Bubba testifies against them in a fraud case called Bubbawater.

Back here in Bubtucky, we are happier than we've been in years, except for a few soreheads who still like Denny and the Cards, and are jealous of the Big Blue, but just won't admit it.

A full range of activities is planned for Bubba History Month, including a parade and a burping contest.

We won't keep you posted.

Wednesday, September 27, 1989

IT'S A SURE BET THAT LEGALIZED GAMBLING'S HERE TO STAY

I used to wonder what the 21st century would be like in Kentucky.

Hey, maybe I already know.

There I am (if I last that long) on a sunny day in 2010 and a couple of kids walk up and look at me.

"Let's ask him," says the 12-year-old.

"OK," says the 10-year-old. "He looks old enough to remember everything."

"What's your question, kids?" I croak.

"Can you really remember when gambling was illegal in Kentucky?" they chorus.

"Sure I can. Back in the old days, gambling was illegal, except that horse racing wasn't gambling."

"It wasn't?"

"Not if you bet at a track. It was only illegal if you bet with a bookie."

"What's a bookie?" asks the 10-year-old.

"They were people who became extinct after the Kentucky Lottery began in the late 1980s."

"I knew that," says the 12-year-old. "We studied bookies in history class last year."

"Did you?"

"Yeah. The teacher said there was a lottery and everybody bet on numbers. Then pro football. Then pro basketball and pro baseball. It was all legal."

"Did the teacher tell you what 'legal' meant?"

"It means who gets the money. Like, when people were betting on football, it was bad if the bookie got the money. But it was OK if the state got the money."

"You're a pretty smart kid. What else did you learn in history class?"

"Well, then after pro sports, everybody was betting on college sports, then high school sports and now ... well, that's what we really wanted to ask you about."

"What's that?" I say.

"Have you heard of Kicking Up A Fortune?" asks the 12-year-old.

"Nope. I don't keep up with things like I used to."

"It's the new state lottery game on junior high soccer," explains the 12-year-old.

"See, I'm on one of the soccer teams and all our parents have bought a lot of Kicking tickets. And we kids are trying to figure out how to control the point spread at our next game."

"Sorry, I can't help you."

"Ask him about T for the Money," says the 10-year-old.

"What's T for the Money?" I ask.

"The new state lottery game on T-ball," the 10-year-old says sadly. "And I don't know anything about point spreads."

"Well, kid, I guess you're out of luck."

"They're building a new casino across from my school," says the 10-year-old.

"Yeah, but he won't live to see it," says the 12-year-old, pointing at me. "It'll take forever. It's a state project."

Saturday, July 1, 1995

■ A 1995 federal investigation that became known as Operation BOPTROT led to the convictions of 16 Kentucky state legislators for accepting bribes from lobbyists. This brought about changes in the state ethics law.

LAWMAKERS CRACK UNDER $3-A-DAY LOBBY LIMIT

Recently the state Legislative Ethics Commission proposed that a lobbyist be limited to spending $3 a day on a legislator.

That is quite a change from the way things used to be done in Kentucky.

Old way: "Rep. Foghorn? Hi, I'm Elwood P. Slick from the Underground Polluters' Protective Association. Can we discuss my group's perspective on HB 27 over dinner tonight? How about some lobster, a bottle of Montrachet and a few hours of lap dancing in Louisville?"

New way: "Rep. Foghorn? Hi, I'm Elwood P. Slick from the Underground Polluters' Protective Association. Can we discuss my group's perspective on HB 27 over a pack of gum tonight? Would you prefer spearmint or Juicy Fruit?"

Get real. You can't lobby anybody on $3 a day. You can't do ANYTHING on $3 a day.

And what if the $3-a-day rule backfires? On some 6 o'clock news of the future, you will see former Rep. Foghorn step out of his attorney's Lexus and walk into the federal building for sentencing, his family plodding bravely beside him.

"Judge,' he will say, "I apologize to the public and particularly to my constituents. Ever since my recent religious conversion, I have asked myself over and over: 'Why did I do it?'

"The only answer I can give, Your Honor, is that I had been cheapo-ed to death by those $3-a-day lobbyists. I couldn't look at another pack of cigarettes or bag of potato chips without wanting to throw up.

"And so, when that guy from the School Milk Price Fixers' Benevolent Association offered me a $20 bribe, I jumped at it. That's right — a lousy $20. An amount of money that I would have laughed at during the BOPTROT days.

"But after all those granola bars, that $20 bill looked as big as a flag. It was too much. I yielded to temptation. Have mercy on me, Your Honor."

Next, the defendant's attorney stands and addresses the court.

"Judge," he says, "before you pass sentence, I hope you'll take into account that my client was suffering from diminished capacity when he took that $20. As a Kentucky legislator at the mercy of more than 600 registered lobbyists in Frankfort, this poor man is a victim of the $3-a-day spending rule.

"During every regular and special session of the General Assembly, he has had to endure Pop Tarts for breakfast, Twinkies for lunch and Ho-Hos for dinner. Not to mention hundreds of cups of coffee. All that sugar and caffeine — both addictive substances — unbalanced his brain chemistry and clouded his judgment.

"Judge, this was a man who used to leave $20 tips — not a man who would take a $20 bribe. Even during the worst of BOPTROT, Your Honor, the basement on a bribe was $400.

"Now, because of the $3-a-day rule, the ceiling on a bribe is $20. That surely can't be what the public intended when it asked for new ethics in Frankfort. No legislator should have to eat Zingers instead of a decent meal at a restaurant. That rule is saving the lobbyists a lot of money, Your Honor, but it's ruining human lives — and this is one of them."

"Yes!" shout spectators in the packed courtroom, applauding wildly. "Justice! Justice!"

"Order!" snaps the judge. "Order in the court! Otherwise, I'll have the bailiff remove all you lobbyists."

Tuesday, May 23, 1995

ELECTIONS AREN'T WHAT THEY USED TO BE

Pencils, key chains, yardsticks, pocket combs, emery boards, hand fans, garden seeds, cookbooks, matchbooks, fish hooks and tiny mirrors to check your looks.

Not to mention $5 bills and half-pints of whiskey to buy votes.

At one time or another, Kentucky political candidates have handed out nearly everything to get people to elect them. The liquor stores were closed by law on Election Day so that fewer citizens would get drunk and kill each other during political arguments.

No wonder that Election Day now seems as sedate as an old house cat taking a nap on a porch swing.

Mostly vanished are the all-day burgoo-and-barbecue feasts and fish fries that every county once had, no matter if the local treasury were as poor as a church mouse.

Vanished are the little cards of fishhooks that a candidate would hand out, saying, "Keep these, friend. If my opponent is elected, he'll raise taxes so high that you'll have to go fishing just to feed your family."

Still sometimes seen are the political posters on the side of every tree and outhouse. "Vote for Billy Bob 'Tater Bug' Doolittle for Constable. Truthful, Mostly Sober and A Veteran."

But long gone are the whistle stops, with candidates speaking from the rear of a train, then rolling on to the next little community down the line to give the same five-minute speech:

"And I told the driver of this train — I said, 'Mr. Engineer, If we miss every other stop, you be sure to stop at Muddy Rock today. Because that's the one place in Kentucky that I don't want to miss. Because Muddy Rock has some of the finest people in the commonwealth. And when I'm elected and go to Washington, I won't forget the help I got from Muddy Rock ... etc., etc."

Gone are a lot of things. Candidates in the 1996 presidential election will probably be saying, "And remember, when I'm in residence at 1600 Pennsylvania Avenue, my door will always be open — but the street will be closed."

Television and the computer have taken most of the colorful atmosphere and a lot of the suspense out of politics.

Candidates today live and die by how they appear on TV and by their 30- and 60-second TV commercials that are packaged exactly like everything else sold on TV, except for the shopping channel, which gives you more information about a pair of earrings than you can get about a candidate.

As for suspense, there's practically none. A computer starts projecting the winner almost before the polls close.

Thirty years ago, it was fun to be packed into a room at a small-town courthouse on Tuesday night and listen to the votes being counted.

One year in a rural Kentucky county, there was a sheriff's race with seven or eight candidates. The candidate who was running last in the pack kept getting a smaller number of votes as each precinct was called out — five votes, three votes, two votes, one vote ...

Finally, the precinct where he had grown up was called and he got zero.

He jumped up in astonishment. "Wait a minute!" he yelled. "My mother votes in that precinct!"

The numbers were checked again. Sure enough, it was still zero. Mom had voted against him.

You don't get laughs like that these days.

Wednesday, January 7, 1987

LAWYER MAY JOKE HIS WAY INTO RACE

You know the new year in Kentucky is shaping up as an entertaining one when it begins with colorful Republican Joe E. Johnson III, 56-year-old lawyer and horseman, talking about running for governor.

The irrepressible Johnson has such a keen sense of humor that it's hard to tell whether he is serious or not.

Here's how the interview goes: Why would you run?

"There's a noticeable void in both parties," he said. "Besides, I'm only half crazy — that gives me a 50 percent advantage on most of the other candidates."

What would your platform be?

"I'd promise not to lie and steal. In this state, that would be revolutionary. People are tired of thieving politicians."

How much money would you raise?

"None. I wouldn't accept donations. I don't want a campaign treasurer, and I don't want to have to fool with filing reports."

Besides having been a state representative and county judge, are there any other qualifications you'd like to mention?

"I'm probably the only man in Lexington who was kicked out of both the Keeneland Club and the Idle Hour (Country Club). That's not a qualification, but it's a pretty good recommendation."

Is it true that you once gave the late financier Garvice Kincaid a speeding ticket when you were county judge?

"He was doing 80 miles an hour down Richmond Road. I followed him right into his garage and gave him the ticket. He paid it, too."

Will your personal life be an issue? Such as the fact that you've been married several times?

"Not at all. That only shows I believe in women's liberation. I personally liberated three."

You had a heart-bypass operation some time ago. How's your health now?

"It's fine. I went up to the pearly gates and saw my creator. No other candidate can say that."

What would your candidacy accomplish?

"I want to give the people a choice and call attention to the issues. I really can't afford to be governor, but I'd do it as a matter of public service."

When will you announce?

"I won't announce. Larry Forgy announced. I'll run."

What if you run and lose?

"I'll say, 'What the hell' and throw a great party. That's what I did when I lost the county judge's race."

Well, there you have it. Joe E. Johnson III for governor? Maybe the only thing more entertaining than listening to him talk about it would be if he would run.

Friday, January 19, 1990

■ In 1990, Gov. Wallace Wilkinson proposed that the state sales tax be extended. The General Assembly later rejected the idea.

SAM SPADE NEVER HAD TO DEAL WITH SALES TAX

I was sitting in my office one day in 1991 and in walks this blonde wearing an Adrienne Vittadini number that looked like it had been sprayed on her by the Seven Dwarfs.

"I need a private eye," she said.

"You're in the right place, sweetheart," I said.

She shook out a cigarette and tapped it on a sculptured fingernail. I leaned forward and flicked my Bic.

She inhaled and blew a cloud of Benson and Hedges smoke in my face.

"What are your rates?" she said.

"Try $100 a day," I said. "Plus tax."

"Plus tax?"

'Yeah. Wally and the '90 budget, remember? It extended the sales tax to private detective services."

Her mouth twisted. "You're the fifth person today who's pulled that routine on me," she said bitterly.

"First it was my lawyer. Then my accountant. Then my broker. Then my architect. And now you."

"I don't make the rules, sister. I'm just a lonely guy going down mean streets and trying to make a living out of other people's dirty laundry."

"And laundry," she said. "The towel and linen service we use at our mansion is charging sales tax, too. Even the limo service that just brought me to this dump of an office charged tax."

"Look," I said, "don't crowd me. I've got enough problems of my own with this tax thing."

She blew another cloud of smoke scornfully in my direction. She half lowered her purple eyelids and studied me like a bug under a microscope.

"What kind of problems could a man like you have?" she said contemptuously.

"You think Sam Spade, Philip Marlowe and Lew Archer had time to fool with taxes? They spent their time on murders."

"I don't know those people," she said. "They sound distasteful. Do they belong to the country club?"

"They lived in California."

"Oh, California. Were they in the horse business?"

"They were private eyes, lady. You ever see a movie called *Chinatown?*"

"Yes, I think so."

"You think so. Well, do you think Jake Gittes could have found out the truth about Evelyn Mulwray if he'd taken time out to keep a set of tax books?"

"I really wouldn't know," she said, putting an ice cube in every word. "And I didn't come here to talk about some Evelyn what's-her-name. Do you want to handle my case or not?"

"OK," I said. "What is it?"

"It's my auditor," she said.

"What about him?"

"I want him investigated. I think he's overcharging me on sales tax."

Wednesday, December 4, 1985

KENTUCKY LAW: BATHING IS OPTIONAL, BUT DON'T DYE THE BUNNY

You've read those stories about funny laws — it's illegal to mistreat oysters in Maryland, and you can't carry an unwrapped ukulele on the streets of Salt Lake City.

A few days ago, The Associated Press carried such a story, and quoted a publication of the North Carolina Center for Public Policy Research that said a Kentucky law requires everyone in the state to take a bath at least once a year.

Well, we doubted it.

After looking at the Kentucky Revised Statutes, we still doubt it.

We did notice KRS 150.330, which says it is against the law to hunt wild turkeys at night.

We saw KRS 437.060, that famous statute that prohibits the use of reptiles in religious services.

And we were impressed by KRS 244.020. It prohibits drinking a bottle of beer on a streetcar. (An easy one to obey; how long has it been since you rode on a streetcar?)

We also paid attention to KRS 217.350. That one says it's against the law to spit on the wall at a restaurant.

And we couldn't help but notice KRS 63.140, which provides that any sheriff who loses a prisoner to a lynch mob is to be removed from office.

Let us not forget KRS 199.590, which makes it against the law to sell your children (no matter how much you might be tempted when they grow up and wreck your car).

Let us also remember KRS 2.030, which provides that "the emblem of the head of a flagstaff used to display the flag of the Commonwealth of Kentucky shall be the Kentucky cardinal in an alert but restful pose."

(That one is violated all the time. It's a scandal how often you see a droopy-looking cardinal atop a flagstaff. The next time you see one, call the cops right away.)

And KRS 150.485, which says you must have a license to sell mud eels, is likewise abused.

Not to mention KRS 258.235. It provides that your unlicensed dog can be shot for trespassing. We see dogs trespass all the time and get away scot free. But maybe they have licenses.

KRS 436.600 says it is against the law to dye baby chicks, ducklings or rabbits, and you can be fined up to $500 for doing that.

KRS 280.070 says that all ferry accidents must be reported. (This has been less of a problem in Kentucky since the bridge was discovered a few years ago.)

And KRS 72.020 says that if you find a dead body, you must report that, too. (More red tape; will it never end?)

KRS 252.190 declares infected honeybees a public nuisance. KRS 249.180 says you must cut Canadian thistles growing on your property.

KRS 2.085 designates the gray squirrel as the official state wild animal game species. (Bet you thought it was the wildcat, right?)

Naturally, the laws that we had been counting on to help us in our old age have all been repealed. That's KRS Section 204 — the poorhouse laws.

But we found no law requiring that all Kentuckians must take a bath at least once a year.

However, it's not a bad idea. You might want to try it.

Sunday, July 16, 1989

■ In response to overcrowding in the state's prisons, then-Lt. Gov. Brereton proposed that two inmates share each cell in 12-hour shifts.

JAIL PLAN NO BEDTIME STORY FOR THIS INMATE

Kentucky is so pretty this time of year that it's great just to get out and take a drive and see what you can see.

The other day I was driving through Buffoon County and I saw an old buddy named Dwayne standing in front of the courthouse.

"Dwayne," I said, "what are you up to?"

"Six feet and 225," said Dwayne. (He always was a comedian.)

"Aw, you know what I meant. What are you doing these days?"

"Well, son," he said, "I'm in jail again."

"You don't look like you're in jail."

"I am, though.""How can you be in jail and be standing out here on the street?"

"I'm not just standing here. I'm guarding parking meters."

"Well, how come you aren't in the jail?"

"Because it's Leroy's turn to use the bed." He glanced at his watch. "I don't get the bed for another three hours and 47 minutes."

"What in the world are you talking about, Dwayne?"

"We got a new jailer last election. He's trying out that idea the lieutenant governor had to relieve overcrowding in our penal institutions."

"Is he really?"

"Yep. I get the bed 12 hours, and then Leroy gets the bed 12 hours."

"How's it working?"

"Well, when Leroy leaves, I take down his *Sports Illustrated* swimsuit calendar and put up my *Penthouse* calendar. Then when I leave, he puts his calendar back up and takes mine down."

"I see."

"And Leroy's good about waking up in the afternoon in time to turn on the TV and keep up with my favorite soaps."

"That's nice of him."

"It sure is. Did you know Megan's got leukemia on *Santa Barbara* and Adam's been dressing up in drag on *Days of Our Lives*?"

"No, I didn't know that."

"I wouldn't have known it, either, if it weren't for Leroy."

"Dwayne, how is that you're working outside?"

"We've done all the work we can do at the jail. So they said, 'Dwayne, you go guard meters.' If I see that little red flag pop up, I call the meter patrol, and they give that sucker a ticket."

"What do you do on weekends?"

"Leroy and I get alternate 12-hour furloughs. I like to get my hair styled and go to the tanning bed. Leroy usually goes to the movies."

"I guess you're pretty lucky that you got your 12-hour shift in the daytime."

"Actually," said Dwayne, "Leroy prefers the night shift."

"Why's that?"

"Leroy's kind of ashamed about being in jail. Not as many people see you on the night shift."

"I guess not."

"Besides," said Dwayne, "Leroy had gotten used to working nights. He was stealing wicker patio furniture. That's why he's in jail."

"That's too bad."

"It sure is. Leroy only took to stealing that wicker because he was desperate for money."

"What caused his desperation?"

"He used to be in the horse business."

"Oh. Well, what does Leroy do with his nights now?"

"He guards patio furniture. Leroy's the perfect dude for that. He knows all the tricks."

"Dwayne," I said, "it's been nice talking to you. Try to keep your spirits up."

"Our spirits are high," said Dwayne, "because Leroy and I have something to hope for."

"You do?"

"Yes," said Dwayne. "We're hoping that the lieutenant governor doesn't get too many more ideas between now and 1991."

Friday, June 29, 1990

■ In this allegory, the "king" is then-Gov. Wallace Wilkinson and the "queen" his wife, Martha Wilkinson.

NO FAIRY TALE THIS

Once upon a time in a rather large village of 40,410 square miles, one of the villagers told the others: "It would be good to be king. I wish to be king."

"Why should you be king?" asked the others.

"Because I have the divine spark," he replied.

"What is the divine spark?"

"Gold," he said. "And if I am king, each of you will have chances to have more gold of your own.

"How so?"

"I will institute a village lottery," he said. "If you win, much gold will accrue to you."

"How many will win?"

"Only a few. But for a mere pittance, each may buy a chance to win. Is not a slim chance better than no chance?"

Each who heard this thought secretly: Perhaps it will be I who will win.

"It would be good to have much gold," they said. "But what of revenues for the royal treasury? Will you burden us with such increases?"

"I pledge not," he replied.

"Then for the next four years, you are king!" cried the others.

And there was great celebration in the village, with many flagons lifted in merry toasts and many fine words said.

The new king enjoyed being king. The village lottery prospered.

And yet there came a day when the royal revenues increased.

"Nay!" cried some.

"But 'twas for a good cause," said the king. "It will accrue to the village school."

"Aye!" cried others. "And yet did you not pledge . . . ?"

"It was an unwise pledge," said the king. "I was not yet king when I made it. Having been king, I now am wiser."

"Ah," said the others.

"And being now wiser," the king continued, "should I not be king for eight years instead of four?"

"Nay!" cried powerful opponents of the royal court. "There shall be no vote on that."

"Very well," said the king. "Then when my reign ends, the queen shall become king."

"You jest, your majesty," said many.

"I jest not," said the king. "Have any of you business — road paving or whatever — before my royal court for the remainder of my reign? Then heed you this: There will be a grand party for the queen at 1,000 ducats a head. It would please me greatly to see all of you in attendance."

Many brought their ducats and came to the party.

Each thought secretly: What choice have I? If the queen becomes king, then the king becomes king again, then the queen becomes king again ... well, I could be in disfavor with the royal court forever.

Alas and alack. Unlike other tales, this one has not yet had an ending.

OLD LEXINGTON

Remember Old Lexington? People flocked to stores all up and down Main Street. The Little Inn out on Winchester Road was top draw, popular for its prime rib — and its back-room slot machines. The rich and the famous dined downtown at the Golden Horseshoe. It was fun to drive down U.S. 27 to Chef Sears, until one day the traffic congestion ruined the expectation of good food. There were lively roadhouses and bars reminiscent of a Damon Runyon story. And there was Smiley Pete, the "last town dog," who was loved and cared for and looked upon everyone as his friend. They were all alive in Old Lexington. Now only the ghosts remain.

Monday, September 25, 1989

FOR THESE FOLKS, GOOD OLD DAYS WERE GREAT

It was a 50th anniversary, or would have been if the family business had lasted another 12 years.

In Lexington, a lot of people remember Hymson's Tots & Teens, including its former employees.

About 30 of them held their annual reunion luncheon Saturday at the Springs Inn on Harrodsburg Road.

"We opened in 1939 on Main Street," recalled Maurice Hymson, former president of Tots & Teens. "In those days, a low-priced child's dress cost about 98 cents.

"A department store dress might be $1.98. Well, we didn't carry anything less than $1.98. We had dresses that cost $4 and $6 — embroidered and trimmed with French lace — a lot of money in those days.

"We sold dresses that today would be museum pieces."

"And back then, little girls had to have their Easter bonnets and white gloves," said Evelyn B. Hymson, Hymson's wife, who was in charge of the children's department.

"Every Easter, we'd sell 1,200 bonnets and 1,200 pairs of little white gloves."

Not to mention shoes. Hymson's brother, Sheldon "Cokie" Hymson, who ran the shoe department, can recall crowds so large he'd hand out numbered tickets to keep customers in line.

In those pre-jeans and pre-tennis shoes days, kids — like their parents — were dressier.

Hymson's lasted from 1939 until 1977, when it was sold to a Florida corporation.

In its time, it was one of the leading stores in Lexington. Several generations of children avidly read Hymson's back-to-school catalog to see what they'd be wearing that year — from jumpers to party dresses.

At Christmas, the place would be packed. Besides clothing, Hymson's had a large toy department.

"We had the first charge cards in Lexington," recalled Hymson. "It was a six-store card, us and Embry's, Wolf Wile's, Graves-Cox, Purcell's and Mitchell-Baker-Smith." Hymson's was famous for its personalized service.

"We had wonderful salesladies," said Mrs. Hymson. "We knew our customers by name, kept lists of the items they wanted and telephoned them when something arrived.

"And there was a time, of course, when everything was delivered. You'd spend 35 cents on Red Arrow Delivery just to send a $1 pair of women's hose across town." Clothing trends would start on the East Coast and finally reach Lexington, she said.

"I learned that whatever it was, mohair sweaters or Navy-style pea jackets, if it was a hot item in Boston one year, it would be popular in Lexington by the next season or two, at the latest."

Then, as now, peer pressure dictated fashion among students.

"I can remember," she said, "when our daughter, Barbara, was heartbroken because she couldn't wear loafers. She had bad feet and simply couldn't wear them, but they were the thing to wear that year."

And the current rage among young people for designer labels is nothing new, said Mrs. Hymson.

"Twenty years ago," she said, "I can recall this 12-year-old girl in the store one day, and her mother offered her a choice — a winter coat or an Aigner bag. The child chose the bag immediately." Mrs. Hymson thinks there was a gradual change in retailing after World War II, a shift from store service to self-service.

"So many young women had been living on military posts," she said. "They were used to queuing up in line at the PX."

All these years later, said Hymson, "it is very satisfying to occasionally run across the grandchildren of our former customers."

"That's when I knew it was time to quit," said Mrs. Hymson. "When we began seeing the grandchildren of the children."

Wednesday, January 24, 1990

LITTLE INN RESTAURANT LAID TO REST AT AGE 60

This is an obituary for a little Lexington landmark.

The Little Inn Restaurant building, 60, of 1144 Winchester Road, was razed last week.

"There was a time when it was more than just a restaurant — it was a gathering place," said Steve Wright, who owns Little Inn Liquors next door.

The liquor store, once owned by the restaurant, is the only Little Inn name left on Winchester Road.

Wright said his business would keep the name "until something happens in terms of redevelopment."

"We just tore the building down to clear the lot," said W.E. Burnett of Kentucky Central Insurance Co., the property owner.

"I have no idea what's going to happen to it (the site), but something will."

The restaurant building was put up in 1930 and began life as a small, Prohibition-era roadhouse outside town in the days when the city limits stopped at Liberty Road.

It grew into a crowded, popular place with a free-flowing bar and a jovial reputation.

By 1945, it had a back room filled with nickel slot machines and was known for great steaks and the best bleu cheese salad dressing around — even during World War II, when steaks were hard to get.

Lots of people would have dinner there, then go dance to Big Band music at the Springhurst Club or Joyland Park, two other places that have passed away.

The Little Inn was bought in 1953 by Harold and Mary Glass, who owned and ran it until 1976.

When he bought the restaurant, Glass said in a 1976 interview, it "wasn't anything I was particularly proud of, but every time I got a quarter I tried to improve it."

"I kept running off customers that didn't fit with the kind of place I wanted."

Glass had learned the restaurant trade working for Ralph Campbell, who founded such places as the Golden Horseshoe and the Campbell House.

Over the years, the Little Inn building grew from 1,500 square feet to 6,000 square feet.

Its buffet was popular, but its trademark was its prime rib. That was what most people noticed first when they drove past the restaurant — a large painting of a prime rib on one side of the building.

The building closed in 1983, and later was renovated and reopened.

It never completely recovered, though, and failed to find a place among the "theme" restaurant buildings in a city that had grown much larger.

It had a good run. Sixty years is a long time for a restaurant building.

No funeral services were held, other than a few people passing by who watched the place go down.

In lieu of flowers, send memories.

Monday, November 30, 1992

BOOTS' BAR NEVER LACKED COLOR

Once upon a time, the 100 block of South Broadway was more than a canyon between two hotels.

There was no Triangle Park, no Lexington Center.

Downtown was the teeming center of life, and at 115 South Broadway was Boots' Bar, named in honor of its owner, William J. "Boots" Dineen, who had inherited the place from an uncle in 1948.

In those days, Boots' Bar was like something out of a Damon Runyon story. It was a popular lunch spot and horseplayers' hangout where banker and bookie might sit cheek to jowl in front of corned beef sandwiches and bottles of beer.

There was a back room where poker and rummy games were played by the regulars. The room also had copies of the *Daily Racing Form*, scratch sheets, slip sheets and a door with three panels of one-way glass; those inside could see out, but those outside couldn't see in.

It was said that a person might lay down a bet on a horse there.

A comical police raid in 1954 caught the color of the place. The cops charged in just after midnight one Saturday in May, and Dineen insisted they read the warrant to him as the law required.

While the lengthy warrant was being read, police could hear noise and scuffling in the back room. When they finally got in there, they found the room full of smoke, an exhaust fan still running, empty chairs, empty tables and two jokers from two decks of cards.

The officers of the law spied a fresh-looking crack in the wall. They tugged on that part of the wall and it opened. It was an old swinging door, hinged at the top.

They went up a dusty stairway. Upstairs in bed they found an employee of the bar, known as "the Swede."

In the room with him were seven men in hats and coats. An eighth man was found hiding nearby.

"What are you men doing here?" demanded the cops.

No one answered. The question was repeated. One man finally said: "We're visiting the Swede — he's sick."

The police, with no evidence, had to return to headquarters.

There were other raids. Once Dineen was arrested and went to trial. But after a dozen character witnesses — including two bank presidents, eight prominent business owners and even an assistant chief of police — testified in his behalf, the jury simply couldn't reach a verdict.

In the 1970s, Boots' Bar changed hands and locations. It moved to 700 South Broadway where it became a raucous honky-tonk with go-go dancers and a locally famous, left-handed, upside-down guitar player named Little Enis (real name, Carlos Toadvine). The empty building is still there behind the east wall of the South Broadway underpass.

But nothing is left of the old, original Boots' Bar downtown. Nothing except ghosts trying to pick the daily double.

Tuesday, August 10, 1993

MEMORY OF SMILEY PETE LIVES BEYOND SNYDER BLOCK

When I heard that the Ben Snyder block has a rendezvous with a wrecking ball, the first thing I thought about was Smiley Pete.

Pete was Lexington's last town dog. He belonged to everybody and to nobody.

The Ben Snyder block was part of his turf. He used to hang out at Main and Limestone, where he'd have hamburger and waffles for breakfast at Brandy's Kitchen.

Pete mooched all his food. He had a way of baring his teeth that looked like he was smiling, hence his nickname.

For lunch he'd have a bowl of draft beer at Elliston's Turf Bar on North Lime and two or three Hershey bars at Paritz's Short & Lime Liquor store.

Every day at 4 p.m. he'd show up at Carter Supply on West Short Street, where somebody would give him a dog biscuit and a bowl of water. At night, he'd stop by the Opera House, in those days a third-run movie theater, where he'd eat popcorn and more candy.

Pete was part spitz, part shepherd, part birddog and part unknown. He had black fur with some white in it.

People took care of Pete. At Welch's Cigar Store on Main Street he got regular baths. Once, during a rabies scare, downtown merchants chipped in and raised money to send Pete to a kennel until the scare had passed.

Pete had some education. On pretty days, he'd walk over to the University of Kentucky campus. Sometimes he'd see an open classroom door and wander in.

Everybody would laugh, but he'd be allowed to stay.

Pete had some civic pride. He'd be cleaned up and a ribbon put on him to be a mascot for March of Dimes and Red Cross fund drives.

That was a long time ago. Pete died in June 1957. His friends buried him under a big sycamore tree next to the Thoroughbred Record building on North Broadway. His gravestone said: "Smiley Pete — A Friend to All and a Friend of All."

For years there was a brass plaque in the sidewalk at Main and Lime with Pete's picture on it.

As I get older, I see ghosts.

Sometimes when I drive past the Ben Snyder block, I think I see something out of the corner of my eye. Something dark with a flash of white.

Saturday, April 15, 1995

Historical Markers

Back in the days when the Zebra Bar was a large lounge with a horse-shoe-shaped bar, a bandstand and an entrance on West Short Street, Lexington nightlife had its landmarks.

The Zebra that vanished this week was only a shrunken ghost of itself. Even its memory was a relic. Over the years, it had gone from night club to street tavern and finally to oblivion in a pile of dust.

And so there'll be one more parking lot for cars to squat and drip their oil.

Because the Zebra was in a 120-year-old building, it got more attention than most of the other local night spots that have disappeared in the march of time.

We are looking at a yellowed copy of the old *Lexington Leader* from April 1951.

On the entertainment page is a big ad for the Rock House "theatre club" which was featuring exotic dancer Peggy De Soto ("the best deal since Gypsy Rose Lee"), Buddy Wragg's music, Lippincott the magician and Francine the "beautiful xylophone artist." The cover charge for all that entertainment was 98 cents, and students got in for half price on Wednesdays and Thursdays.

The Rock House was a roadhouse on U.S. 25 between Lexington and Clays Ferry. Anyone who has driven that old road in times long past might remember the ruins of the big stone house and what was left of its neon sign.

It was on the west side of the highway. After the Rock House closed, the empty building stood there for years. Hardly anyone noticed when it disappeared.

If you were a boy and you rode past the place with your uncle, he would tell you all kinds of extremely interesting stories about the Rock House — but not if your aunt was in the car.

Closer in to town on Richmond Road, where Lakeview Shopping Plaza now stands, 25 years ago there were places like Brock's —"Where the stars come out," was the motto — and Marty's, where rock 'n' roll legends such as Jerry Lee Lewis and Bill Haley and the Comets performed.

But the most infamous forerunner of those places was the Donagene Club, which was in the same locale 40 years ago.

The Donagene Club was a private club, but hardly exclusive. Membership cost $5 and the annual dues were $1. The place was a former drive-in restaurant that had turned into a rowdy "bottle club" and beer joint favored by young people. It was frequently in trouble with the law.

Its mark in history is a dubious one. The Donagene Club was the site of the largest police raid in Lexington history. The cops took two busloads of prisoners to the old jail on Short Street.

So many of those arrested identified themselves as "John Smith" and "Jane Smith" that one of the deputy jailers remarked: "It looks like we've got the whole Smith family here."

On the other end of old U.S. 25 was the Green Dome, a roadhouse between Lexington and Georgetown on the east side of the road. There is no telling how many teen-agers once lied to their parents about where they were going and sneaked off to the Green Dome. The long-vacant building, complete with its old green tarpaper dome, is still standing.

Like the Zebra, such places have no historical markers.

In Lexington, if you can remember names like Joyland, Danceland, the Palms, Club La Flame and the Limehouse you're the historical marker.

Saturday, December 30, 1995

How to Know When You're Old

An old year ends and a new one prepares to arrive. Before the champagne pops, the paper hats crumple and the band plays Auld Lang Syne, more than 30 ways to know you're growing older in Lexington:

■ You remember when New Circle Road was not a circle, but an arc, and was called "the Beltline."

■ You once celebrated New Year's Eve at the Firebird Lounge in the Phoenix Hotel.

■ You danced to music from a band called the Mag Seven.

■ You saw Babe Parilli throw passes at Stoll Field and watched Cotton Nash shoot baskets at Memorial Coliseum.

■ You rode the Wildcat roller coaster at Joyland Park.

■ You went to the Ben Ali when it was a theater instead of a parking garage.

■ You used to eat lunch at the Canary Cottage.

■ You listened to Artie Kaye on local radio and watched June Rollings and Ted Grizzard on local TV.

■ You remember when there was an airport called Cool Meadow on Newtown Pike.

■ You remember when celebrities Elizabeth Taylor and George Hamilton went to the races at Keeneland and had dinner at a restaurant in Chevy Chase called The Bistro.

■ You remember when UK won the NCAA basketball championship and fans wrecked the Bluegrass Airport terminal welcoming the team home.

■ You used to get a nickel cup of coffee at Jerry's Restaurant.

■ You went bowling at Wildcat Lanes.

■ You remember when Lexington had only one television station.

■ You used to rock and roll at Danceland on Old Frankfort Pike.

■ You remember when there was no "castle" on Versailles Road.

■ You remember when the "castle" on Versailles Road was not for sale.

■ You used to get double dips at Hughes Ice Cream.

■ You went to the wrestling matches at Woodland Auditorium.

■ You remember the wall murals at the Golden Horseshoe and the Stirrup Cup restaurants.

■ You were on the train that got stuck in the snow on the way back from the UK-Tennessee football game.

■ You went shopping at Purcell's and Stewart's and Wolf Wile's.

■ You remember when Man o' War was exhumed and moved to the Kentucky Horse Park.

■ You went to something new in town called a "theme restaurant." It was named Nellie Kelly's.

■ You drove your car into one of the biggest things on Main Street; it was called Dick Webb's Mammoth Garage.

■ You bought a hamburger at Lexington's first McDonald's. It was on New Circle Road near Eastland Parkway.

■ You bought a ticket to see Elvis at Rupp Arena. He didn't make it.

■ You watched a Hollywood stuntman try to jump from the top of Kincaid Towers and survive. He was killed.

■ You once played on a miniature golf course downtown.

■ You remember when there was an upstairs bowling alley downtown. Pins were set by hand.

■ You remember when Adolph Rupp had his own La-Z-Boy recliner to sit in at Rupp Arena.

■ You heard Little Enis, whose real name was Carlos Toadvine, play the guitar upside down and sing at the Zebra Bar.

■ You saw artist Henry Faulkner drive around town in his Cadillac filled with dogs, cats and goats.

■ You promised yourself you would never grow old in Lexington.

And yet somehow you did.

Tuesday, May 13, 1997

ATTEMPTED LYNCHING IS ALSO PART OF HISTORY

This is Historic Preservation Week in Lexington. There are tour festivals, awards — everything you might expect — all around town.

Gold ribbons tied in big bows decorate historical markers at the Fayette County Courthouse.

Something happened on those courthouse steps. Something Lexington has tried to forget for nearly 80 years.

On Feb. 9, 1920, a lynch mob of white men stormed those steps, knocking aside an Army machine gunner.

They wanted to lynch a black man named Will Lockett. He had confessed to killing a 10-year-old white girl named Geneva Hardman.

Lockett was on trial for murder inside the courthouse. Threats of a lynching had caused the governor to ask for help from federal troops.

Such threats were not idle. In 1919, the year before the Lockett incident, 83 persons had been lynched by mobs in the United States.

That didn't happen in Lexington.

When the mob, firing guns, charged the courthouse, soldiers and local officials fired back.

Six people were killed and about 50 were wounded.

But there was no lynching.

As one would expect, the shooting drew an enormous amount of national publicity.

It was called the first case south of the Mason-Dixon Line where a lynch mob had been stopped by fire from troops.

It was a terrible day, and yet, in a way, it was one of Lexington's finest hours.

The rule of law had prevailed over the rule of mob violence.

More than 25 years after the Lockett incident, Joe Jordan, city editor of the old *Lexington Leader*, wrote in the *Atlantic Monthly* of February 1946 that: "... the mob picked the wrong town for a lynching party. Fayette County had not seen a lynching in 50 years. It didn't see one then, and it hasn't seen one since."

Jordan had witnessed the incident. He wrote: "Thousands of outsiders flocked to Lexington on the day of the trial ... some (from Alabama) disclosed to reporters that they had made the long trip to have a part in the expected lynching.

"They misjudged the temper and underestimated the courage of the county officials, who had issued plain warnings that anyone attempting to take the prisoner from them would be killed."

Lockett was later electrocuted for the murder of the Hardman girl. But the Lockett incident had sent a message to the rest of the country.

The message was that lynchers were cowards who wouldn't stand up to hot lead.

That was the title of Jordan's article: "Lynchers Don't Like Lead."

All these years later, there are many historical reminders — festooned with gold ribbons this week — at the Fayette County Courthouse.

Out in the yard and inside, in the corridors, there are markers for soldiers killed in war, politicians, judges, crime victims, statehood anniversaries and even a marble slab that tells you the name of the contractor who put the plumbing in the building in 1899.

There is not a marker or a single word about the Lockett incident of 1920.

Was it nothing of historical value worth preserving? Not even the idea behind it?

Time has changed one thing.

Ironically, the front steps where the mob rushed up to death now end only at an empty marble foyer and a sign on a closed front door that reads:

"For security reasons, except in cases of an emergency, this door should not be used."

Saturday, July 26, 1997

A PRETTY DRIVE OR THE ROAD TO RUIN?

One of the most pleasant drives out of Lexington used to go south on a two-lane road past sprawling, green farms with clouds sailing across the sky.

You could see an old mansion or two, set back from the road, secluded behind huge trees and well-tended lawns where lightning bugs sparked in the dusk.

Some people took the drive to have dinner at a country restaurant called Chef Sears.

The place had knotty pine paneling, a gun collection on display (the chef's hobby) — and culinary specialties such as "Gypsy steak," made with pickles and onions and served in its own little skillet.

Chef Cornelius Pete Sears had quite a following in the old days.

He had been chef at the Phoenix Hotel, and then at the Golden Horseshoe, a hangout for horse people, including Hollywood actor Don Ameche and director John Huston.

When Sears opened his own restaurant on that two-lane country road, the place was so quiet that, at night, you could hear the crickets over the hum of automobiles on U.S. 27.

That was Nicholasville Road as it once was, a pleasant drive out of town to a roadside restaurant or a drive-in movie.

Now it's the worst drive in town — a working model of how overdevelopment can destroy a city corridor's ambience and replace Gypsy steak with a million greasy burgers.

And the worst drive in town is going to get even worse than worst (somebody really needs to invent a new superlative to describe the clogging of Nicholasville Road).

The Urban County Planning Commission this week voted unanimously to let developers throw up another Wal-Mart, another Lowe's and six other businesses on 43 acres at the northwest corner of Nicholasville Road and Man o' War Boulevard.

This land was once part of the University of Kentucky's South Farm, which hosted horticultural research and protected the land for scenery and greenery.

It's a different shade of green now — the shade of cash. UK sold the land to the developers this year for $18.4 million.

In other words, don't leave the old home place to UK in hopes of saving it.

Big Blue will turn a buck as quickly as anybody.

It will be interesting to see how the Urban County Council will vote this fall on adding even more development to the most congested road in the county.

It is merely annoying to sit in jammed traffic.

But if you have seen a serious wreck on Nicholasville Road during heavy traffic and watched as even the emergency vehicles have trouble getting through to the scene, it's appalling.

Will this latest development be rubber-stamped by the Urban County Council, or will someone on the council question whether one more Wal-Mart outweighs factors such as human safety and common sense?

Nicholasville Road couldn't remain a nostalgic dream, but does it have to be even more of a suburban nightmare?

The enjoyment of driving into or out of Lexington has dropped considerably over the years.

There was a time when Lexington was a sort of Emerald City because of its surroundings.

It was a horse town, but it was farm country. And it had a genuine greenbelt that you could reach from downtown in five minutes.

It won't be that way again. But what will it be instead — and how much worse?

Wednesday, December 24, 1997

A REMEMBRANCE OF THINGS PAST: THE GOLDEN HORSESHOE

Christmas Eve — yet for some reason I'm thinking of an old address that doesn't exist anymore: It was 129 East Main Street.

You won't find it in the 1997 Lexington City Directory. It hasn't been there for years and years.

There was a time when 129 East Main would have been packed on Christmas Eve.

It was a restaurant and cocktail lounge called the Golden Horseshoe.

Famous people had dined there. Some of them were depicted in a big painting on one of the restaurant's wall.

It was a scene that showed George Swinebroad, the Keeneland sales auctioneer, taking bids on horses.

The bidders in the picture included a local horse buyer who bore a striking resemblance to movie star Don Ameche.

The real Ameche was one of the regulars at the Golden Horseshoe when he was in town to buy thoroughbreds.

Visiting celebrities were often wined and dined at the Golden Horseshoe.

When film director John Huston came to Lexington to shoot scenes for a 1950 movie called The Asphalt Jungle (today a film noir classic), he said he wanted to try the regional cuisine.

Huston was served a plate of country ham at the Golden Horseshoe. Other diners couldn't believe what he did next — he smeared mustard all over his country ham.

As I write this, I'm looking at some old images from the *Herald-Leader* library.

There's the old place itself with its big, lighted horseshoe on the front of the building. Its entrance awning is stretched out over the sidewalk.

The town was much smaller then in terms of population and suburban sprawl.

And yet somehow, in the old pictures, 129 East Main looks more sophisticated than the night spots that are here today.

One photo termed "an unusual guest" shows a 20th Century-Fox publicity man named Eddie DeAngelis and a actress named Theona Bryant seated at a table.

Between them sits a 5-year-old cheetah named Flo. Bryant is smiling and wearing a dress that matches the cheetah.

All three were in town to promote a 1954 movie called *The Egyptian*.

The movie was pretty awful, but the old photo is great. It captures what the place was, a sort of Lexington version of the Stork Club.

Ralph Campbell, who later built the Campbell House on Harrodsburg Road, was the creator of the Horseshoe.

Before that, the 129 East Main location had been a popular eating and drinking spot called Keith's Bar & Chop House, an Irish-flavored hangout with Damon Runyon-type characters.

A colorful personality named Joe Keith ran the place. Keith's slogan was: "Good food is not cheap, cheap food is not good."

Campbell, who made the place more upscale, had a talent for publicity stunts.

Here's another old Horseshoe photo. This one's from a front page in 1951.

"Londoners and Lump-Sum Rations," says the caption.

It shows three visitors from England admiring a huge steak at the restaurant.

The point of the picture was the food shortage in England in the years following World War II.

That one steak, the British visitors said, "would represent the meat rations of four people in London for a week."

There will be no Christmas Eve party at 129 East Main this year. Like the steak, it's all gone.

Friday, April 24, 1998

Progressive Politics and Tall Tales

Inside the Woodland Grocery front door with the "Hatred Is Not A Family Value" sticker on it, past the silent Donkey Kong machine and across from the shelf of old Dan Fogelberg and Cat Stevens record albums, Don Pratt talked about the closing of his store.

"I'm still not sure what I'm going to do after this place closes," he said.

"It's been my life for 26 years. Maybe I'll finally write a book about my prison experience — about being a political prisoner in America."

The 1960s flashbacks were beginning to close in at 201 Walton Avenue this week. You can't separate this place and its owner from the '60s.

Pratt, 53, is closing his neighborhood grocery on June 1, after 16 years in the store's original location at 496 East High Street and 10 years on Walton.

The store was started in the early 1900s by Winfield S. Duncan.

Besides a grocery, Pratt says, it's a forum for "progressive politics and tall tales."

Every day about a half-dozen regulars show up to talk issues, tell jokes, drink Vernor's Ginger Ale and eat $2 country ham sandwiches.

Pratt was one of Lexington's best-known protesters during the Vietnam War years.

In a way, it's the key to his life and the key to the style of Woodland Grocery.

I helped turn that key in 1967 when I was a reporter interviewing local protesters leaving on a bus to a national rally in Washington, D. C.

I asked Pratt whether he was going to publicly burn his draft card like many others at the rally.

"No," he said, "it's already been burned." That was against the law. After his quote appeared in the newspaper, the FBI came looking for Pratt.

He eventually served 20 months in a federal correctional facility in Milan, Mich., as punishment for resisting the draft.

Some saw him as a wild-eyed radical. He saw himself as a Presbyterian acting on conscience.

After his release from prison, Pratt bought the Woodland Grocery in 1972 for $7,500 and started a new chapter in his life. It turned out to be a long chapter.

"I never thought I'd be a grocer," he said. "My father was the director of purchasing at the University of Kentucky and my mother was a nurse.

"I had wanted to be a teacher. But of course, that was impossible. I was classified as a convicted felon."

Declining business is the reason for closing the store, he said.

"Too many convenience marts open 7 a. m. to midnight. I can't match those hours."

The foster children need time, too. Two boys live with him now. Pratt has opened his home to 39 of them in the past 11 years, including one he adopted.

He also has a 22-year-old daughter, a student at Western Kentucky University.

He lives on Walton Avenue across the street from the grocery. It's the house with the '55 Plymouth Belvedere in the driveway, an acquisition from one of his home-delivery grocery customers who moved to a nursing home.

A lot of people know Pratt today as a political gadfly at government meetings. He twice ran for Congress, and once showed up at City Hall to protest flooding by wearing a scuba-diving outfit, flippers and all.

His former spouse, Kathy Pratt, was a 3rd District Urban County Councilmember from 1992 to 1996. "I tried not to embarrass her," he said, "but I probably did."

We talked about the old days. They seem so far away now. There is no draft to resist, and the little wars that Pratt protests now are things like zoning changes.

He's a board member of the Central Kentucky Chapter of the ACLU, a member of Citizens For Ethical Government, board coordinator for Amnesty International and the Family Resource Center at Crawford Middle School.

Craig Hoffman, a traffic signal repairman and one of the "Woodland Club" of lunchtime regulars said: "I go there for the intellectual stimulation, the boring gossip and the bad jokes."

He seriously described Pratt as "a very sensitive, compassionate individual who cares about the common concerns of people" then jokingly added: "And a corny son of a gun."

When a politician stops by for a sandwich, Hoffman said, "It's no holds barred on what we talk about — whether it happens to be Brereton Jones, Bob Babbage or whoever."

On Wednesday morning this week, the first customer at Woodland Grocery was Earl G. Robbins, 90, who came in to get a dozen eggs.

Pratt went to a cooler to get them for him.

"He's a thinker," Robbins confided. "And if you think, you get into trouble."

Wednesday, September 23, 1998

The Stopover Stomp, Where GIs Romped

Forget for a moment that famous poetic stuff about a loaf of bread, a jug of wine and thou beside me singing in the wilderness.

Instead, think of an old piece of sheet music, a ghostly piano playing with a bounce on the Esplanade and hepcats swinging in the wilderness of World War II-era memory.

In the key of F, here it goes: "Down in Lexington, Kentucky, there's a new dance that is ducky.

"It's a serviceman's invention — COMPANY ATTENTION!

"Come on and get goin', time, babe, you was knowin'

"That new G.I. romp... they call the STOP-OVER STOMP!"

Heaven knows how many old novelty songs have been written about Lexington and are lost and forgotten.

But this one, a paper antique rediscovered last week in a relative's collection of sheet music, caused me to think of one of Rod Serling's old *Twilight Zone* TV shows.

It was a story about a man who discovered an antique radio that still worked.

But when he turned it on, it began picking up broadcasts from the past, sentimental old songs that were on the airwaves when the radio had been new.

That's something of what I felt when I looked at the words and music of *Stop-Over Stomp*.

The sensation was like listening to Lexington in 1944, the year the song was published.

The old Stopover Station — local history books don't use the hyphen in "stopover" — was on the west side of the Esplanade downtown.

It was an English Tudor-style building that stood where the Bank One parking garage now stands on the one-block street between East Main and East Short.

It was a USO-type canteen, a home away from home for visiting soldiers, sailors, Air Corps and Marine Corps personnel who drank coffee, socialized and danced to the Big Band music of the time with local volunteers.

Or, as the song puts it in the slang of 1944: "It's easy to master, stomp slow then stomp faster ... Sing, Joe, while you swing, Joe ... plank down your dogs, then hop like frogs."

(Note to younger readers and mouse potatoes: "Joe" is G. I. Joe, "dogs" are feet and this song is probably not on the Net.)

The words and music of *Stop-Over Stomp* were written by Maury Madison.

The song was published by William Renick Smith, who, in 1944, lived in The Britling, a rooming house at 434 South Broadway.

The price of the sheet music was 35 cents.

The jitterbug and stomp dancing at the Stopover Station embodied the vibrancy of downtown in that day and time.

The place was so lively back then that some of the people who lived through that era told anecdotes about it for the rest of their lives.

Over the years, I've heard a lot of stories about the Stopover Station.

Across East Short Street, in a space where the Central Church Apartments stand today, there was outdoor dancing, too, back in the G. I. Joe days.

The Big Band sound of the Esplanade vanished, and in the 1950s the street was better known for its upscale shops.

As old downtown faded into a smaller-than-life image in the rear-view mirror of history, so did the Esplanade. The building that housed the Stopover Station was demolished about 1972.

Today the street is better known as the sedate location of the Lexington Club, the oldest private club in town.

Somewhere, time's jukebox is still playing the music of Glenn Miller and the Andrews Sisters, but not on the Esplanade.

—LEXINGTON CHARACTERS

"We have a city now," a Lexington woman once said. "What I miss is the town." What she really missed were the "town characters." In the long ago of sainted memory, everybody knew the devoted hospital orderly, nicknamed "Sweet Evening Breeze," who donned an evening gown after dark. More recently, Bradley Picklesimer's notoriety as a drag queen made him the subject of a documentary and earned him a career as a Hollywood party decorator and nightclub operator. Roger Ware acquired the wisdom of the streets, because that's where he survived — and lived. And J.W. Davis Sr., who built much of Chevy Chase, was never in a hurry to die and lived to 91. Behind his desk a sign read: "It's Better to Be Late At the Golden Gate Than to Arrive in Hell On Time."

Wednesday, April 8, 1998

LEXINGTON HAD CHARACTER WHEN IT WAS JUST A TOWN

Virginia Harris, 77, moved from Cynthiana to Lexington in 1937 and remembers when downtown was thought of as "everybody's neighborhood." She's writing a memoir of Main Street regulars from the old days. While we talked during a recent interview, she brought out a photo of Everett "Lost John" Booker.

"He was my favorite of all the town characters," Harris said. "He created more joy than anybody I ever knew here."

I told her I remembered him, too. Lost John was a street entertainer who played his harmonica for tips in the courthouse yard.

Sometimes he had a jug band with him. Sometimes he carried advertising signs on his front and back. Not big ads. Stuff like "Eat at Joe's."

He wore a stovepipe hat, huge bow tie, swallow-tailed coat and a rubber snake around his neck.

He entertained thousands a few at a time, not just in Lexington, but in the surrounding towns of Central Kentucky, where you usually saw him standing in front of a movie theater to work the incoming and outgoing crowds.

"When he died," Harris recalled, "I went to his funeral at the Charles Haggard Funeral Home.

"I was the only one there. No one came, no one called. There was no preacher."

There may be something of that poignancy still inspiring Harris. The booklet she's writing will give recognition to people who were familiar, but not famous.

"There was Callahan the Cop," she said, "and Little Eddie, who sold newspapers at Main and Upper streets. 'PAPER!' You could hear him all the way to Broadway.

"And Tom Lee, who had a Chinese laundry on North Limestone Street. I can still see him in his round black hat and his long white jacket, his hair in a queue.

"And Charley, who sold ice cream from a cart. And the blind man who played the guitar in the courthouse yard.

"There was Charles Ben Williams, 'Walking Ben' we called him. He had a long, white beard and hair to match, wore overalls, carried a shepherd's crook and walked barefoot everywhere he went — even in cold weather."

She remembers some of the old bookies, too, guys with names like Slick

Bill and Gus the Greek.

"If you saw a bookie come into the Metropolitan (restaurant) and shake hands with the doctors and lawyers eating there, well... that's how the money was passed."

But she said she wasn't going to write about the gamblers in her booklet because "I'm so opposed to gambling."

In 1997, Harris published a 23-page booklet through the Carnegie Center for Literacy and Learning.

It was called World War II Memories.

That one was about her memories of Lexington during the war years.

Harris began writing in a class she attended at the Carnegie Center after her husband, Walter Harris, died. He was a city bus driver; she is a retired bookkeeper.

Besides the old Main Street characters, she said, there's something else that she misses about Lexington.

"We have a city now," she said. "but what I miss is the town."

Tuesday, March 21, 1995

SWEET EVENING BREEZE

In this space last week, we wrote about the corner of Main and Limestone streets and some colorful downtown characters of days gone by.

Several readers called to ask: "How could you leave out the most famous Lexington character of all —James Herndon?"

Well, it's true. In his time, Herndon was more than a town character. He was a Bluegrass personality. Even out-of-towners recognized him as they drove down Main Street.

Most people didn't know his name. They knew him by his nickname: "Sweet Evening Breeze."

Herndon was a man who wore women's clothing. These days, drag queens are a dime a dozen, but to the Lexington of the 1940s, Herndon was a sort of pioneer in that particular area of personal appearance.

Evening was his dress-up time. To see him promenading down Main Street in a sea-green evening gown was quite a sight. It almost stopped traffic. People tooted car horns and pointed and waved. In those days, few men wore pancake makeup in public.

Herndon was the almost legendary subject of stories, jokes, anecdotes, poems and at least one song.

According to one of the most popular stories, a rookie cop spotted Herndon dressed up on the street one night and promptly arrested him. The cop figured that anyone looking THAT much out of the ordinary must be in violation of some city ordinance or other.

But when the cop got Herndon to jail, he couldn't figure out what to charge him with — so he asked the jailer what to do. The jailer was a man named Dudley Veal, a town character himself who was renowned for butchering the king's English.

"What'll we charge him with, Dud?" asked the cop.

"Aw, hell," said Veal, "just charge him with being a proverb!"

(Veal was trying to say "pervert" but the cop was so thoroughly confused by then that he let Herndon go and decided to forget the entire incident.)

That was a long time ago. But even by the often intolerant standards of that time, Herndon was remarkably well tolerated in a Lexington that was a much smaller town where people were more likely to cross paths.

Herndon was a good citizen who cared for many residents in their times of illness. He worked nearly his entire life as an orderly at Good Samaritan Hospital.

He had grown up at the hospital. When Herndon was a child, he suffered an eye injury. An uncle who was transporting horses took Herndon to Good Samaritan for treatment.

In a 1967 interview, Herndon recalled that "the next morning (my uncle) went off with the horses in the horse car and left me here." The hospital superintendent took him in and raised him like an orphan.

"I began to take the hospital's mail route," he recalled, "and I used to go around to patients' rooms and play this little ukulele. Of course, I only knew one song."

He began working at the hospital for $4 a week when he was about 14. It was not an easy life. He worked every day and his only time off was two Sunday afternoons a month.

When the hospital honored Herndon in 1967 for 40 years of service, he had been there longer than anyone else on the payroll.

James "Sweet Evening Breeze" Herndon, who loved to bake cakes and wear dresses, died in 1983. If he were around today, he would scarcely recognize the old downtown that he once startled.

Saturday, March 26, 1994

BRADLEY PICKLESIMER

If this story had a title, it would be: THE BIGGEST HAIR IN HOLLY-WOOD.

Back in the 1980s in Lexington, when Bradley Picklesimer showed up, you could almost hear Wild Thing playing in the background.

In a word, he was outrageous.

He was the town's most famous two-fisted drag queen. He ran a show bar on Main Street called Cafe LMNOP where he was also the bouncer — and hey, you haven't really been bounced until you've been thrown out of a bar by a guy wearing blusher and six-inch heels.

He was also the subject of a documentary film called *Bradley Picklesimer* that played in New York to favorable critical reviews.

My theory is that New Yorkers, who are bored by anything less than a serial killer, were trying to figure out exactly what Bradley was. He is not what you might call a stereotypical Kentuckian.

After a well-publicized "estate sale" — as he called it — Bradley (whom everybody calls by his first name) went away to Hollywood.

That was in 1991. I called him this week and asked him what his new life is like. Here's what he said: "It's just wonderful. The earthquakes here are better than any amusement park ride I have ever been on.

"I came here three years ago with $300, a bag of clothes, a pair of high heels and a dream. People here think a Hollywood agent made up my name. When I dress in full regalia, they pay me for personal appearances. 'No,' they say, 'you can't be from Kentucky.' I tell them the truth is stranger than fiction.

"Even in Hollywood, I still actually have the biggest hair. I tell 'em it's a Southern tradition — the bigger the hair, the closer to heaven. And I have a total-see-through chain-mail outfit that is amazing. If people knew that under that makeup is a 37-year-old hillbilly, they'd be astounded.

"I may be getting older, but my waist is getting smaller. It's down to 24 inches. Looking fabulous is everything out here. When I told my family I was moving to Hollywood, they weren't a bit surprised.

"The money spent on lavish parties here is unbelievable. I do party décor for a living, you know. Every Hollywood movie prop that has ever been used is still out here in some prop warehouse. It's wonderful.

"I did the *Sunset Boulevard* premier party (the new Andrew Lloyd Webber musical) at Paramount and got to work on the same sound stage that Gloria Swanson did the original movie on. It totally gave me chills to be there doing that.

"I'm going to be working on the Jean Claude van Damme wedding. It'll be a very elegant Victorian garden style.

"I just did the Paul Mitchell wedding — you know, Paul Mitchell Hair Care products — and the flowers alone cost $250,000. Roger Daltrey sang to the bride, Wolfgang Puck did the desserts and Cher was a gate crasher.

"And I have a club. When my friend, Billy Limbo, passed away, his Club '70s fell into my hands. Madonna picked out the people to be in her *Deeper and Deeper* video from our club. We play nothing but '70s music. Sara Gilbert from Roseanne hangs out there.

"But what I really like to do is garden at home. It's very beautiful here. There are hummingbirds everywhere."

Monday, April 4, 1988

J.W. DAVIS SR.

On his 90th birthday, J.W. Davis Sr. gave me a sly wink and said, "You know the only good thing about being old? You can get away with anything."

Davis died Saturday. He was 91.

The Chevy Chase neighborhood won't be quite the same without his Cadillac — always a shiny, new one — parked in front of his office at 857 East High Street.

Davis had built a lot of that neighborhood and several others in Lexington.

Beginning in the 1920s, he built hundreds of houses, including the little building that housed his real estate office, back in the days when that part of Chevy Chase was still a dairy farm.

"Don't talk to me about farming," he'd say. He had been raised on a farm and could remember driving cattle on foot across two counties.

The rural life held no charm for him. That was why he'd gone into building and real estate.

He had his little trademarks. At restaurants, he always tipped with silver dollars.

And he handed out thousands of gold-colored fingernail clippers with his name on them like a calling card.

When the first American woman astronaut, Sally Ride, visited Lexington, Davis made sure she got a pair of those clippers.

He was fascinated with volcanoes. When Mount St. Helens erupted, he got on a plane and flew out to take a look at the thing.

"We almost went right down into the crater," remembers his granddaughter, Robin Doller, who went with him on the trip.

Davis had been a pilot during World War I in an era when "you carried a pair of pliers, a screwdriver and plenty of baling wire."

He once told his son, J.W. Davis Jr., "If you didn't have three forced landings, it was a slow day."

During an interview on his 90th birthday, he laughed when he recalled enlisting in the old Air Corps when flying was such a risky business.

"The first thing you did," he said, "was sign a paper telling them where you wanted your body sent."

After the war, he had a couple of auditions with Hollywood studios.

He was more interested in photography than acting, but he'd thought that making movies "would be non-stop action. After I saw that you stood around waiting most of the time, I lost interest."

In his later years, people would ask him how he'd lived so long. He would point to a sign on the wall behind his desk.

It read: "Don't Worry. Don't Hurry. It's Better To Be Late At The Golden Gate Than To Arrive In Hell On Time."

John Woods Davis Sr. was a genuine Lexington character.

They're going to miss him in Chevy Chase.

Tuesday, October 6, 1998

JOHN B. WARNER

"My childhood memories?" said John B. Warner, 62, very ill and with death waiting quietly outside the door for the slightest invitation.

"Well, honey, they aren't exactly ordinary. My father was one of the owners of the Lookout House, a big Northern Kentucky nightclub full of showgirls and gangsters in the 1940s.

"I was too young to hang out with the gangsters, so I hung out with the showgirls."

He smiled at the recall of it.

"They'd baby-sit me backstage and let me play with their sequins and eyeshadow and the brightest red lipstick. And of course, those glorious wigs that looked as big as pup tents.

"I must say I took to it all like a little duck to water. By the time I was 5 or 6, my father was worried about me. He bought me a cowboy outfit to 'make me more masculine.'

"When I came downstairs wearing it, I had the hat and guns on right, but I had taken those fur chaps and thrown one over each shoulder like a fox stole.

"My mother looked at my father and said: 'I don't think this is going to work.'"

Warner died Friday after heart surgery at Central Baptist Hospital. He was buried yesterday, wearing an Armani suit, at Hillcrest Memorial Park. About 25 people attended the graveside service.

His mother had been right about him not changing. "Military school didn't work, either," he said. "I was the only cadet drawing dresses."

Warner was still at home when interviewed earlier this year.

Home was a one-bedroom apartment crowded with paintings, statuettes, Louis XVI-style chairs with the gilt flaking off, cold steak chateau briand in the refrigerator, 200 pairs of shoes, a mountain of silk underwear and a molehill of money in the bank.

He was in dire straits. He had lost one leg to diabetes, the remaining foot was probably going to be amputated, his heart was failing and he was still trying to get some work as a decorator who had once studied in New York.

He had designed store windows in the old Lexington downtown days, home interiors for rich horse people, mall windows for McAlpin's. He had designed everything from party dresses to pawnshops.

"Social-climbing doctors' wives are the worst to work for," he said. "I'd rather design for coal miners."

He hoped to be remembered as a designer. Some of his friends thought he would be more remembered as a teller of outrageous tales that skewered everyone, including himself.

They were hilarious portraits etched with acid. A sample: "She'll have to have her next face lift at the Urgent Treatment Center. And that scarf looks like something she was wearing 20 years ago during Yves St. Laurent's gypsy look."

When a Lexington socialite's elderly husband died and left her $100 million, he said thoughtfully: "Honey, if I had that much money, why, I just wouldn't die. I'd refuse to."

"You can get the best gossip in town just by listening to the messages on my answering machine," he said.

His one-liners were locally famous: "I've given up love for food and I've never been happier," he'd quip. "At least a chocolate chip cookie never asks you for money."

His last big party was the 1997 Madden Derby Eve bash. He attended in a wheelchair.

The year before, he was there, too. He had designed some of the runway dancers' costumes and wanted to see them.

He had seen a lot of gay Lexington history in his time.

He could remember when men were arrested for dancing together in the 1950s, and when movie star Rock Hudson sang around the piano bar at The Gilded Cage (now The Bar) on East Main Street in the 1960s.

His family never accepted his lifestyle, Warner said. When he was dying Friday, a friend, Bob Morgan, rushed to the hospital.

"John had been such an outsider all of his life," Morgan said. "I thought he wouldn't want to die alone."

Friday, March 31, 1989

ROGER WARE

When Roger Ware died this week, part of the Lexington street scene went with him.

Ware, 48, died early Wednesday from injuries received in a car crash on West High Street.

He was a passenger in the car.

That figured. Most of his friends couldn't remember him ever owning a car.

More likely, you'd see him on a bicycle or on foot.

And always on the streets.

In a city surrounded by bluegrass, the downtown pavement was his turf. And the down-and-out people of downtown were his constituents.

When he ran a short-lived campaign for mayor of Lexington in 1977, you'd see him "holding court" each morning in the coffee shop of the old Greyhound Bus Station on North Limestone Street.

A steady stream of street people would stop by to ask his advice on all kinds of problems.

This was a decade before "street people" and "helping the homeless" became standard planks in political platforms.

He loved the streets — the gossipy bars, the bizarre characters — and he'd take time to talk to everybody.

He had been a waiter, a barber, a masseur, a cosmetologist, a kitchen worker and a dozen other things.

He had been beaten and robbed numerous times, but he could laugh at his misfortunes.

In fact, one of his favorite stories was about the time he was robbed and left in a field out in the country in the middle of the night.

"And I mean left, honey," he'd say. "They took everything — even my clothes."

It turned out he'd been dumped on a cattle farm. A bull chased him across the field until he dived over a fence to safety.

After that incident, one of his friends nicknamed him "the midnight matador." He was capable of the outrageous.

Years ago, he once performed that socially improper, teen-age prank known as "mooning" — and he did it from the window of a Cadillac at the socially proper High Hope Steeplechase.

He could be a loyal friend or a devastating critic. He had been kicked out of some of the worst bars and invited to some of the best parties.

He wrote many letters to lonely people in prison. In return, they'd send him what he called "real Kentucky crafts," such as wallets cleverly made of empty cigarette packages woven together.

Once he told me a story about hitchhiking through South Carolina.

After a long stand in the blazing sun on a highway between Columbia and Charleston, at last a carload of "good ol' boys" stopped to give him a lift.

"Can you chip in any money for gas?" they asked him.

"Now, I don't have any money," he said. "But I can pay for my ride by entertaining you.

"How about if I recite Molly Bloom's soliloquy from (James Joyce's novel) *Ulysses*?"

That was vintage Roger, all right.

One of life's hitchhikers. As we all are.

The ride finally ends for everybody

SEND-OFFS

Don Edwards once said, "Everybody who dies is in somebody's memory." Death often makes clear how much the individual touched the lives of those who knew him. It reminds the living of what they have lost — and of what they have left to lose. This section of farewells brings together a wide-ranging fraternity — George W. Headley, Carlos Kearns, John Y. Brown Sr., Dr. Eslie Asbury, "Shipwreck" Kelly, Robert Penn Warren, Reece Holloway and Rufus Lisle. What unites them is their special meaning for Edwards. They are gone, but for Don, and now for the rest of us, their memories live on.

Wednesday, February 6, 1985

GEORGE W. HEADLEY

Blanche: "I don't want realism. I want magic. ... I try to give that to peo-
ple. ... I tell what ought to be the truth." — *A Streetcar Named Desire.*

It might be a Chinese ivory cricket cage. He would add gold and emer-
alds, transforming it into a one-of-a-kind cigarette box.

Or he might take a slab of malachite and turn it into a diamond-studded
obelisk. A rare seashell would become a pearl-encrusted conversation piece.

George W. Headley was witty, elegant and talented. And his bibelots
were his pride and joy — his art was his magic, for, like the fictional Blanche
DuBois, he was an incurable romantic with an unfailing sense of style.

The French word "bibelot" means an object whose value resides in its
beauty and rarity.

Headley, who created enough of these miniature rarities to justify his
own museum, once remarked that he hoped someone would say of him after
his death that "he left the world more beautiful than he found it."

"George put the chic in Lexington," said a longtime Headley friend, "and
he did it with a sense of humor."

This past November, when Headley was named to the local Social
Registry's first "best-dressed list," his response was vintage:'

'It was my accessories that got me on the list," he said. "Lots of fake leopard shoes and other leopard accents, including the upholstery in my Mercedes."

Then he confessed that he was still wearing suits and topcoats tailored
for him by Brioni of Rome in 1962, adding, "Who can afford Brioni these days?"

Once he had truckloads of sand delivered to his LaBelle Farm on Old
Frankfort Pike to build a picturesque beach by the lake.

That was also a time of Sunday night suppers that Headley gave —
steak-and-kidney pie with an excellent red wine, the supper sometimes inter-
rupted when his dozen dachshunds upstairs began yapping loudly.

He knew Kentucky, where he was a member of a very old, very prominent Bluegrass family of gentleman farmers, thoroughbred horse fanciers
and landowners.

And he knew the world. He had studied art in Paris, designed jewelry
in California for the families of Hollywood moguls Louis B. Mayer and David
Selznick, traveled widely and had been part of the social scene of New York
and Palm Beach with his late former wife, Barbara Whitney.

Besides jewelry and bibelot design, he loved archaeology, landscaping and oil painting. And he loved showing off the museum he had founded; in 1978, he unlocked the doors on a Memorial Day holiday just to give movie actor Gig Young and Young's fiancee a personal guided tour of the place.

Headley had an irreverent, wonderful sense of humor. Once he painted a surrealistic portrait of two Lexington friends.

"Oh, don't worry about it," he told them when they decided not to buy the painting, "I'll change the faces and sell it to someone else."

And he did.

An unforgettable last image of him was in the hospital during his illness. He was sitting in a wheelchair, wearing his opal-colored mink coat, cradling a bottle of champagne and saying, "Let's pop the cork!"

And in a final postscript of style, he had told friends and relatives: "When I go, I don't want sadness at my funeral. I want there to be champagne and dancing."

Wednesday, April 30, 1986

CARLOS KEARNS

I remember that summer in Madison County, how the pickup truck would come into town early to get you, the sun barely up, the streets quiet.

The green tobacco, cut and speared and heavy with dew, was waiting out there on the farm to be loaded on the wagon and hung in the barn. You wanted to get started before it got too hot.

On the way, the truck would stop to pick up the others standing on lonely corners or sitting on sagging porches, lunch bags in hand.

One of them was a lean, muscular man, bronzed dark as an Indian from working outdoors, eyes bleary from nights of beer drinking in the rough taverns of east Richmond.

He was known to carry a gun. "Nobody pushes me around," he'd say.

His name was Carlos Kearns. He would have been in his mid-40s then; that was almost 30 years ago, long enough ago that the passenger trains were still running through Richmond. We used to hear their faraway diesel horns while we were working together in the tobacco field.

Kearns died last week at 73 — an old man who walked with the help of a cane — and died notoriously, as the central figure of a spectacular murder case in which two women are charged with killing five people.

He was shot three times in the head, he was stabbed, burned and run over with his own car. Even then, his heart kept beating an additional two hours before he was declared brain dead and the machines were turned off.

I can believe he'd have been a hard man to kill. I remember him from that summer our lives intersected; I was the town kid working on my brother-in-law's farm, he was one of the men picking up a few dollars helping house tobacco. Even in middle age, with the booze and the cigarettes, he was as strong as whipcord.

He held himself aloof from the other farmhands. He had been an officer in the Air Force, he reminded them. He could talk engineering, hydraulics, carpentry. He'd point out a warped joist in the barn roof and curse the green wood that had caused it; if the tractor stalled in the heat of the day, he'd lecture the rest of us on vapor lock and carburetors.

"If you're so damned smart, what're you doing housing tobacco for $12 a day?" one of the others would ask him.

"I don't need the money," he'd say.

"I'm just here to show the rest of you sons of ———- what a real man looks like."

They kept their distance from him, didn't challenge his brags. As he said, he wasn't a man to be pushed around. But he was prone to go where people might try; honky-tonks where the beer was cold, the jukebox loud and there was sure to be a fight before the night was over.

He was intelligent. But he also had some dark, moody streak in his mind that kept him on the wild side of life.

"You're always reading," he said to me one day. "What is that?" We were sitting in the shade just inside the barn. It was lunch break: bologna sandwich and a banana. I showed him the paperback book *On the Road* by Jack Kerouac. Everybody my age was reading it that year.

"What's it about?"

"These two young guys looking for kicks. They hitchhike all over the country. You know, beatniks."

That would get him off on a war story or a hobo story or a barroom story of his own, always some anecdote in which he was the hero.

You never knew how much of it to believe, but he sure looked as if he could have done some of those things.

I was to run across his name in later years. As a Lexington police reporter, I'd see it on the blotter — for being drunk or being in a brawl or "carrying concealed a deadly weapon."

"I used to work with this guy," I told a cop once. "He's smarter than this."

I told him about the farm.

"Well, maybe he oughta live on a farm by himself and stay away from indoors," the cop said. "That's when he seems to get into trouble. Maybe he's just not an indoors kind of guy."

Then I was older, a night city editor. Every now and then I'd write a headline on a story about Carlos Kearns. They were always two-bit, inside-page stories; usually about a disturbance at some North Limestone Street tavern.

More years passed. A lot of them. Nothing changed until last week. I picked up the paper and saw on the front page that Kearns was dead. All this came back to me then. Everybody who dies is in somebody's memory.

Kearns was buried yesterday at a national cemetery in Jessamine County. I know that place; it's on what used to be the main road but now is a side road bypassed by a bigger highway.

It's out in the country, too. That's the only part of it Carlos might have liked. As the man said, he probably was not an indoors kind of guy.

Tuesday, June 18, 1985

JOHN Y. BROWN SR.

The gray hair was thinning on the leonine head, but the wit had stayed razor sharp through most of a century — and Kentucky lost a storytelling lawyer of the old school when John Y. Brown Sr. died this week.

One of his best was about the time a client accused of stealing a pig came to him for defense.

"Well," Brown said, "did you steal the pig?"

"Yes, sir, I did."

"Where is the pig?"

"Cleaned and dressed and in my refrigerator."

"All right," said Brown, "now here's what I want you to do — go get half the pig and bring it over here and put it in my refrigerator."

When the case came to trial, as Brown told it, there he stood before the jurybox, booming in tones of indignation: "Ladies and gentleman, I've known this defendant for 20 years — and I can absolutely, positively guarantee you that this man doesn't have any more of that stolen pig in his refrigerator than

I have in mine."

Or he'd chuckle about the time he arrived in a Kentucky mountain county to defend a client accused of murder. As he walked into the courthouse, he noticed a group of tobacco-chewing, teen-aged boys also headed for the courtroom.

"Why aren't you boys in school?" he asked them.

"We skipped yesterday," one replied, "to see if old John Y. Brown can save that no-good S.O.B. from the 'lectric chair."

Then he'd laugh about how circumstantial evidence was sometimes the strongest evidence — and tell about the Kentucky defense lawyer who asked the prosecution's witness: "So, Mr. Jones, you didn't actually see my client bite that man's ear off during the fight, now did you?"

And Jones replied: "No sir, but I saw him spit it out."

Or the time the notorious Southeastern Kentucky bootlegger, carrying a large brown-paper bag, came to Brown's home in Lexington and asked Brown to defend him.

"I'll need a retainer," Brown said.

The bootlegger dumped the grocery bag, which was full of $5 and $10 bills, out on Brown's kitchen table.

"Now, Mr. Brown," he said politely, "just prove I'm not a bootlegger and I'll give you the second bag after the trial."

Gamblers are dreamers, and Brown, who loved poker and horse racing, enjoyed telling about how he'd dreamed — "clear as day, I could see the number as it crossed the finish line" — which horse would win the Kentucky Derby two years in a row.

The first year he had the dream, he bet on another horse and lost. The second time, he bet on the horse he'd dreamed about and won. And then he'd bemoan: "But I never had that dream again. If I had, I could have won a fortune on the Derby."

Before a storytelling session of anecdotes and dreams was over, however, Brown, his eyes turning dim with memory, would sometimes include one nightmare — an Eastern Kentucky murder case in which the defendant was from a wealthy family.

The family of the young girl who had been killed had hired Brown as a special prosecutor.

Brown lost the case.

"He was as guilty as sin," Brown said, "but I found out too late that the jury had been bought off. That case has haunted me more than 30 years. It'll be with me the rest of my days."

Monday, September 12, 1988

DR. ESLIE ASBURY

Dr. Eslie Asbury, who died last week at age 92, was one of the best storytellers in the horse business.

"It's easy to make a small fortune raising thoroughbreds," he'd say. "Just start with a large fortune.

"That's like the rich man who asked his banker if there was any money in the horse business. And the banker replied: 'There will be if you go into it.'

"Well, I always remembered that story. About 50 years ago, my banker advised me to sell my horses and buy bonds. I never took his advice."

He had bred many stakes winners — including Determine, the 1954 Kentucky Derby winner — at his Forest Retreat Farm in Nicholas County and was the first Kentuckian elected to the Jockey Club.

"Tell me some secrets," I said, the last time I interviewed him. He was 91 and, after 75 years of smoking, had given up cigarettes the year before.

"What do you want to know?" he said. "I'm too old to have any secrets left.

All I have is honors — that's what you get after all those who knew the truth about you are gone."

"What's the secret of success?" I asked him. "And of longevity?"

"Genes and luck," he said. "Everything else is very minor, both in life and in the horse business."

He had, he said, never thought he'd live so long.

Someone once asked him how he'd felt when he woke up on the morning of his 90th birthday.

"Surprised," he said.

That was vintage Doc Asbury, all right. He didn't pull punches.

"Old people must not expect to be happy," he told the Lexington Rotary Club during a speech in 1985.

"Happiness is an illusion of children and crazy people. Healthy retirees ought to go to work, at least part-time."

Money, he said, was "not that important, as long as you have some. No matter how rich you are, you can exist in only one room at a time and eat only three meals a day."

Being a medical professional, he used to say, could be almost as financially risky as being in the horse business.

Then he'd tell one about a physician who visited a rich Kentucky woman who'd called him because her maid was sick.

The doctor examined the maid, and there was nothing wrong with her.

"I know that," said the maid, "but I won't get out of this bed until she pays me my salary. She hasn't paid me in two months."

"Move over," said the doctor. "She hasn't paid me in two years."

A lot of people will miss Doc Asbury.

Wherever he is, we hope there's a mint julep and a good 3-year-old in the barn there with him.

Friday, September 5, 1986

JOHN SIMMS "SHIPWRECK" KELLY

You might see him, still big and bulky, at Commonwealth Stadium on some autumn afternoon with crayon-colored leaves and a slight chill in the air. He would be in town for a visit, and somebody would take him to the football game.

To the young people in the crowd, he was an old man that other old people were making a mysterious fuss over. And if the young people wondered who he was, they didn't wonder for very long — they were there to see the game, not museum pieces.

John Simms "Shipwreck" Kelly, 76, died last month in relative obscurity in Lighthouse Point, Fla.

That fact was of scant interest to anyone but sportswriters, who dug up Kelly's old yardage-gained figures from the UK football history books and gave him the standard farewell that Saturday's heroes of a half-century ago always get in Kentucky.

Kelly hadn't been front-page news since June 30, 1941, when his wedding at the Ritz Carlton Hotel with Whitneys and Vanderbilts in attendance was on front pages all across the country.

He had married Brenda Diana Duff Frazier, 20-year-old heiress to a $3.5 million trust fund, New York's 1938 "Debutante of the Year" and the toast of what used to be called "cafe society" in a time when "Glamour Girl Weds Gridiron Star" was the sort of headline you would expect on the Kelly-Frazier nuptials.

Years later, some people insisted that a famous short story by Irwin Shaw called *The Eighty-Yard Run* was inspired by Kelly's life. It was a story about an over-the-hill football hero who never recaptured in life the magic that he had once enjoyed as an athlete.

Whether he inspired Shaw or not, Kelly was a specimen of American life and the stuff of which Hollywood movies might be made.

The scenario would go like this: Small-town boy from Springfield, Ky., becomes idolized running back on state university football team and big man on campus, falls in with the local horse set, climbs in society like a salmon swimming upstream, plays pro ball in New York and marries an heiress.

After that, you can write your own finish to the story. In Kelly's case, there were years spent in high society, a job as an investment banker, trophies won as an amateur golfer, a divorce from the heiress, another marriage, another divorce, old age and finally death.

A few other headlines and photographs are sandwiched in there — Kelly credited with saving lives during a hotel fire in Rome; an Italian playboy beaten up by New York police while being thrown out of the first Mrs. Kelly's Park Avenue apartment; pictures taken in Europe, Bermuda, Saratoga, etc., wherever it was fashionable to be at the time.

Make of it what you will. Only Kelly himself could have told how full or empty a life it turned out to be.

Thirty years later, however, he made sure that a UK football biographer understood that he had worked undercover for the FBI during World War II — he said he was still concerned that some people might think of him "as the draft-dodging football hero who married the heiress."

He simply didn't qualify for the military, he said, because he broke a leg that never healed properly while playing catch football with a grandson of movie director Howard Hawks.

I remember talking with Kelly a few years ago. He was in town for a funeral.

"One of the girlfriends from the old UK days," he said.

"What's your life like now?" I asked him.

"Rather quiet," he said. "I live on Long Island in Jock Whitney's old boathouse. He left it to me in his will. I was the only non-Whitney mentioned. And I have real estate investments in Florida."

A moment later, he said something I'll probably remember the rest of my life.

I had asked him some question about those old days, some obscure point of fact that the reference books weren't clear about.

He thought a long time, but couldn't come up with an answer.

"I'm sorry," he said. "I simply can't remember. Do you realize how many parties I've been to since then?"

Sunday, September 17, 1989

ROBERT PENN WARREN

If Robert Penn Warren had been born five miles farther south, I wouldn't be writing this column and you wouldn't be reading it.

He would have belonged to Tennessee instead of Kentucky.

Warren, 84, who died Friday, lived more than 60 of his years outside the state. I can think of no one else who was, at the same time, so barely and so thoroughly a Kentuckian.

He was born and raised in Guthrie in Todd County, barely above the Kentucky-Tennessee state line.

But his novels were full of Kentucky history.

Night Rider was based on the Kentucky "tobacco wars," when growers tried to organize to get market parity for their crops.

The Cave was based on the famous Floyd Collins case of 1925. *World Enough and Time* was based on a 19th-century Kentucky murder case.

Band of Angels was based on a 19th-century Kentucky incident in which two young women who had been born free of a white father and black mother were sold into slavery at public auction after their father died.

Even *All the King's Men*, based on Louisiana Gov. Huey Long, had a historical flashback that was set in Kentucky.

"You once said that 'all of a child's vital images and attitudes are formed by the age of 5 or 6,'" I once reminded Warren during an interview.

"So wouldn't it follow that all of your vital images and attitudes are Kentucky images and attitudes?"

"I suppose it must," he replied.

He was an old man then, his large-boned face buckshot with freckles, his red hair faded to silver.

"Writing," he said, "is simply a person trying to show what he feels and thinks about living. The deeper you search inside yourself, the better the writing."

He didn't think much of writing courses. "The best course in writing," he said, "is a good course in Shakespeare."

And the best way to appreciate poetry, he said, is "by immersing yourself in it and letting it talk to you."

There was no secret, he said, to the actual work of literary production.

"For me, it was locking the door, taking the telephone off the hook, fixing a big pitcher of iced tea and sitting down at the typewriter."

Kentucky was always more impressed by Warren's honors than by his work.

He was the most distinguished writer ever born in Kentucky, but there is no Robert Penn Warren High School in any of 120 counties.

He won three Pulitzer Prizes, including two for poetry, but I have never met a Kentuckian who could quote a single line of his poetry.

The U.S. Congress named him the national poet laureate. The Kentucky General Assembly never got around to calling him state poet laureate.

He was a classicist in an age of pop culture, a master of language in a civilization that had increasingly turned away from books and turned toward film and video.

He was celebrated, but not a celebrity. He was not outrageous like Truman Capote and not political like Norman Mailer. You might rarely see him on PBS, but never on *The Tonight Show*.

There is much debate about education in Kentucky these days.

It is worth noting that Warren — Rhodes scholar, Yale University professor and one of the most highly educated Kentuckians of his century — was a child who was read to, not propped up in front of a TV set; a child who was reared in a home where books were valued and used; and a child who grew up connected to his family, his community and his state by a strong tradition of oral history.

He transformed that upbringing into honored American literature.

Even so, he said, human existence "remains a mystery. We are born to sin, suffer, repent and die. What can be said beyond that?"

Thursday, September 19, 1996

REECE HOLLOWAY: FLY HIGH IN BLUE SKIES, OLD SOLDIER

Here was how a morning would begin, Reece Holloway told me: The American prisoners would line up in front of their barracks for inspection while the Nazi guards watched.

The commandant of the prison would walk up and down the lines, smoking a cigarette in a holder and looking at the prisoners. His face was cold and expressionless; it was a face you couldn't read.

As his cigarette burned down, the tension grew.

With no warning, the Nazi commandant would draw his Luger pistol and shoot a prisoner in the head.

The man would fall, almost dead by the time he hit the ground.

It was a random thing. If you were a prisoner, you woke up every morning wondering whether today would be your day to die.

And that was the point of it — to inspire terror.

All that was long ago. But the war never seemed more real to me than when Reece, who was my father-in-law, told me that story.

He had been a captain, a P-38 pilot shot down over occupied France and burned by the flaming oil from his fighter plane.

He survived the burns. His captors moved him to Germany, where he survived again. After the war, he came home to Lexington, went back to school at the University of Kentucky on the GI Bill and went back to the Air Force as a flight instructor during the Korean War.

He worked as a tobacco buyer and rose to become president of a company, traveling the world over as a passenger in first-class airlines instead of as a pilot of a P-38.

The war stayed with him in small ways, though. For the rest of his life, he couldn't abide the sight of turnips or cats. The prisoners had been forced to eat both in that Nazi camp.

Reece's day to die was this week. On Tuesday, he breathed his last, finally ending a nearly 30-year war of his own with multiple sclerosis.

His doctor and nurses at the VA Hospital on Leestown Road cried when Reece died.

He had been quite a jokester and had been there a long time. Once, he and another VA patient had gotten into an argument and then a grumpy-old-men fight — crashing into each other with their wheelchairs.

The World War II vets are passing. Their 50-year celebrations are over, and Bob Dole will be the last of his generation to be nominated for president.

Life won't seem the same without them. For my generation, they were the guardians of our childhood who saved us a world to grow up in.

Who can imagine Dwight D. Eisenhower not being a general or John F. Kennedy without PT 109?

And the famous photo of the Marines raising the flag on Iwo Jima. In school here, kids were proudly taught that one of those Marines was a Kentuckian.

Something in our heart still longs for guardians. Why else would Colin Powell and Norman Schwarzkopf be two of the most popular people in the country? Besides Reece, I think about some of the other hospitalized vets I met:

The infantry sergeant who had a leather holder full of Bronze Stars and other medals, but no visitors.

The Army nurse who had trekked across Africa and told so many funny stories.

The bombardier who still felt guilty for the times his plane couldn't reach the target and he'd let the bombs fall anyway to lighten the load and get out of there alive.

"If they hit orphanages or hospitals, I didn't know," he said. "But it's on my soul. Isn't it?"

And Reece ... well, I like to think of him in his P-38 again, flying a cloudless blue sky with no enemy and no end, amen.

Tuesday, March 4, 1997

RUFUS LISLE

Rufus Lisle definitely had his 15 minutes of anonymity. When he died last month, he was sort of an anonymous poet laureate of Lexington.

The obituary of Lisle, 87, was as solemn as one would expect for a former president of the Fayette County Bar Association, a member of its hall of fame and one who served on the commission involved in the merger of city and county.

And yet this same Rufus Lisle was also the author of:

All Kappas wear designer clothes,
And so they thought it crude
For one at U. of K. to pose
For Playboy in the nude.
 The good sisters at Beta Chi
Did not condone this sin;
The culprit they did vilify
By snatching back her pin.

Whether it was a college student being kicked out of a sorority for baring all, or the county attorney ordering police to raid a play called *Oh! Calcutta!* at the Lexington Opera House, Lisle had a keen eye for local folly.

He turned it all into satiric verse, but made sure he didn't sign his name to any of it.

In Lexington social circles of years ago, he was famous for a much-circulated poem about the Blue Grass Debutante Ball of 1961.

It began:

Buy me a bid to the Ball, Mom,
Part with a bundle of pelf;
Buy me a date of my own, Mom,
I sure want to get off the shelf.
I want to display all my lines, Mom,
For the boys who are loaded to see,
So cough up five hundred in cash, Mom,
Or I fear an old maid I shall be.

In 1997, how many readers would know that "pelf" was a once-popular term for "money" and that $500 in 1961 was more like $2,500 today?

"Rufus' verse was kind of a humorous sidelight to local history," said Burton Milward, Lexington journalist and historian.

As a prominent lawyer, Lisle probably wrote anonymously "because he didn't want to be sued," said his son, Charles Lisle.

A more complete collection of his poetry is expected to appear later this year.

In its way, Lisle's poetry is social history. It captures what people in a much smaller Lexington once talked about and laughed about, but now is mostly forgotten.

For example, a police chief named E.C. Hale ordering his officers to shave their sideburns inspired Lisle to write:

Our City Hall was all a-buzz
With sounds of disbelief;
There'll be no fuzz upon the Fuzz
As long as Hale is Chief!

Not all of the poems are from a Lexington of decades ago. Lisle went on writing into the 1990s, and his targets include recent follies of politicians and horse breeders.

In a Lexington smaller than today's, many people must have known of Lisle's authorship.

One indication is that when a famous writer of humorous verse, Ogden Nash, came to town for a lecture, Lisle was chosen to introduce him.

Lisle did it in rhyme, of course, and noted in his introduction that Nash's mother had been a Kentuckian.

In his lecture that night so many years ago, Nash said that humor was something we cling to in our struggle against the centrifugal force that is trying to fling us into outer space.

With the passing of Rufus Lisle, we have slipped a little closer to that edge of darkness.

Monday, February 4, 1991

PETE AXTHELM

Suddenly the hero saw that the living, too, are dead, and that we can only be said to be alive in those moments when our hearts are conscious of our treasure; for our hearts are not strong enough to love every moment.
— From *The Woman of Andros* by Thornton Wilder.

When sports commentator Pete Axthelm, 47, died Saturday of liver failure in a Pittsburgh hospital, one of the signs of Derby time in Kentucky went with him.

Whether he was writing for *Newsweek* or talking into an NBC television camera, "Ax" had been a part of the Derby scene for years.

He would stay as a guest at Hamburg Place Farm, where he'd figure the morning line on the afternoon croquet games, dash up to Louisville to do a TV "remote," be back in time for the fashionable parties and still manage to squeeze in a visit to the Chevy Chase Inn, a hole-in-the-wall tavern where he liked talking to the regulars.

He was a Yale University graduate whose first book had been about existentialism and whose second was a biography of jockey Steve Cauthen.

He had come to Kentucky in the 1970s to write an article for *Esquire* magazine about the wild frolics of Derby week in the Bluegrass. He liked it so much that he came back every year.

Once I asked him: "Why do we look for heroes in sport? Is it because we can't find them elsewhere?"

"Remember what (Ralph Waldo) Emerson said about 'the only thing that can bring you peace is the triumph of principles,'" he said. "That's what we're secretly longing to see in a horse race or an NFL game — the triumph of some principle."

Once he asked me: "Stopped drinking, huh? What does the world look like to you?"

"It's like *The Wizard of Oz*. Remember how everything is in black and white until Dorothy leaves Kansas? Then it's all in color. When you stop drinking, you just never leave Kansas."

"I love that one," he said, laughing. "I'll use that one sometime."

He liked gambling, liked the celebrity status that came with being on TV. He liked knowing famous entertainers such as Willie Nelson and Jimmy Buffett.

He said that he was never unhappier than when he'd undergone a period of sobriety. He said he had decided to keep drinking.

"I've had a good life," he said. He slid from *Newsweek* to *People*, from NBC to ESPN.

I wish that things had turned out differently for Ax.

I wish that I could see him again this Derby.

I wish that he had chosen to live in Kansas instead of to die in Oz.

ACKNOWLEDGEMENTS

Lexington Herald-Leader

President and Publisher: Timothy M. Kelly

Editor and Vice President: Pam Luecke

Managing Editor: Tom Eblen

*   *   *

Production Staff for *Life is Like a Horse Race*:

Editor: Art Jester

Copy Editor: Ami Shaw

News Researcher: Linda Minch

Cover Artist: Camille Weber

Designer: Epha Good

Picture Editor: Ron Garrison

Mascot: Smiley Pete

About the Author

L exington Herald-Leader columnist Don Edwards was born in Corbin and cut his teeth on a drumstick at Colonel Harland Sanders' original restaurant so long ago that the Colonel had dark hair, no goatee and looked like an ordinary human. Edwards sat next to Harvey Lee Yeary in English class at Eastern Kentucky University. Yeary changed his name to Lee Majors and became a famous Hollywood "Bionic Man." Edwards didn't change his name and in 1964 became an obscure newspaper reporter. By 1971, he was city editor of the old Lexington Herald. He became a full-time columnist in 1978. His work has appeared in The Atlantic Monthly and he has won numerous Kentucky Press Association awards, including three first-place awards for column writing.